INTRODUCING THE TEACHER-LEADER/DESIGNER

GUIDE FOR SUCCESS

LOUIS L. WARREN
WILLIAM A. SUGAR
EAST CAROLINA UNIVERSITY

KENDALL/HUNT PUBLISHING COMPANY
4050 Westmark Drive Dubuque, Iowa 52002

Cover image credits are as follows:
Woman with boy and Hispanic woman courtesy of Comstock.
All other images courtesy of Photos.com.

ISBN 978-0-7575-1954-3

Printed in the United States of America

10 9 8 7 6 5

Contents

The Conceptual Framework of Teacher-Leader/Designer

Chapter 1

Teachers Are Leaders

This chapter will introduce and discuss Teacher Leadership. The concept of Teacher-Leader is a critical piece of the theoretical framework of Teacher-Leader/Designer. This chapter will define Teacher Leadership and its characteristics. A Teacher-Leader possesses many different leadership roles, from within the classroom to beyond, and these roles will be explored and discussed. At the end of this chapter, readers should know what a Teacher-Leader is, how to identify Teacher-Leaders, provide examples of the multiple roles of a Teacher-Leader, identify the characteristics of Teacher-Leaders, and gain insight into the future of Teacher Leadership. Teacher Leadership, with its potential impact on education, is gaining increased recognition in the lives of educators.

After reading this chapter, you will be able to:

1. Define Teacher Leadership.
2. Describe how Teacher-Leaders emerge and the stages of their development.
3. Describe why Teacher Leadership is important.
4. Identify some of the primary roles of Teacher-Leaders.
5. Describe the primary purpose of Teacher Leadership.
6. List the characteristics of Teacher-Leaders.
7. Describe how Teacher-Leaders are selected to fill leadership roles.
8. Describe the desired outcomes of Teacher Leadership.
9. Develop a Personal Professional Mission Statement.

TEACHER LEADERSHIP—WHAT IS IT?

What is Teacher Leadership? A teacher is often defined as someone who instructs, whereas a leader is often defined as someone who influences. Therefore, a Teacher-Leader must be someone who is an influential instructor. For many of us, that definition is obvious, because an effective teacher has always been an influential instructor by guiding students in direction, action, opinion, and outcome.

It is interesting that defining the term Teacher Leadership is challenging for educators even though it is generally agreed upon that teachers are inherently leaders. As Eloise Forster (1997) states, the concept of Teacher Leadership is not new, it is just that as educators, we have difficulty in defining basic terms and concepts that should be inherent in our professional vocabulary. Often, when educators speak or write of Teacher Leadership they do not define what they mean by the term, resulting in confusion or misunderstanding (O'Hair & Reitzug, 1997). Everyone seems to have a different notion of what Teacher Leadership is. What is yours? How would you define Teacher Leadership?

There are several definitions of a Teacher-Leader that have been conveyed by various researchers in the field of education. According to Katzenmeyer and Moller (2001), Teacher Leadership is defined as "Teachers who are leaders who lead within and beyond the classroom, identify with and contribute to a community of teacher learners and leaders, [and] influence others toward improved practice" (p. 5). Teacher Leadership is defined by Pellicer and Anderson (1995) as "the ability . . . to engage colleagues in experimentation and then examine more powerful instructional practices in the service of more engaged student learning" (p. 4). Sirotnik and Kimball (1995) suggest the following definition: "Leadership is the exercise of significant and responsible influence" (p. 4). In this text, we will define Teacher-Leaders as "effective teachers who lead in many capacities, with goals of positive growths and outcomes."

A Teacher-Leader is not an administrator. Too often we automatically consider school administrators to be the leaders. Of course, administrators are leaders, but they are not the only leaders found within our schools. This is becoming more and more the case as teachers play an increasingly significant role in shared decision making, site-based management, teacher-driven curriculum, and staff development (Stone, Horejs, & Lomas, 1997). Teachers are, and can be, very important leaders within the school. Teachers are experts on what is taking place in the classroom, what practices have worked in the classroom, and what practices could work in the classroom in the future. Also, as the student performance and accountability of schools continue to increase (e.g., No Child Left Behind policies), administrators are increasingly turning to teachers on their faculty for help in leading the schools toward excellence (Keedy & Finch, 1994; Clemson-Ingram & Fessler, 1997).

Teacher Leadership is a multi-faceted role. First and foremost, teachers are leaders within the classrooms because teachers are formally responsible for the academic outcomes of their students. Students' achievements are being more frequently measured and analyzed through standardized testing and assessments, and teachers are increasingly being held more accountable for student performance. Teachers are now in a position where they must be able to demonstrate, through valid and reliable measurements, the mastery of content by their students. If students are not meeting expected academic growth, then teachers will face consequences such as remediation on teaching or even removal from the classroom. Thus, it is critical that teachers are able to contribute in significant ways as to how these issues of accountability are addressed and dealt with in society.

Teachers must make many decisions related to what takes place in the classroom, such as setting up the classroom, selecting appropriate teaching and assessment strategies, implementing management strategies, communicating effectively with parents, administrators, and the community, developing Individual Lesson Plans for specific students, and determining what resources to bring into the classroom. In addition, teachers must know and understand the curriculum and the developmental needs of their students, as well as how to differentiate instruction to meet the needs of their students. Frequently, teachers are also responsible for supervising para-professionals serving in their classrooms. As you can see, teachers fulfill many leadership roles and responsibilities and must make many decisions each day.

Outside of the classroom but within the school, teachers assume leadership in such roles as grade level or department chair, mentor, participant on various school committees (e.g., School Improvement Team), and in staff development. Teachers also provide leadership outside of the school by serving on curriculum development teams, consulting, or actively participating in various professional organizations at the state, national, or even international level (Clemson-Ingram & Fessler, 1997). As stated earlier, there are many important leadership roles that teachers fill without being an administrator. Can you think of other leadership roles in which teachers serve?

TEACHER LEADERSHIP—WHERE DOES IT COME FROM?

Teacher Leadership has always existed. As the teaching profession has evolved, leadership has always been inherent in the role of an effective teacher. Even in earlier times, when schools often consisted of one room, the teacher did everything from sweep the floor to making administrative decisions. When multiple teachers were required due to the increased number of students being taught, the school leader was called the principal teacher. Even today, in some job descriptions, it is stated that leadership skills are necessary for good teaching (Gardner, 1989).

Although the concept of Teacher Leadership is not new, only in recent years has it received the attention and recognition that it deserves. Teacher Leadership is a concept that is currently being defined and redefined by educators as they seek to more clearly understand its roles, responsibilities, and possibilities (see, for example, Katzenmeyer & Moller, 2001). It is interesting to note that when teachers are asked to define the leaders within their schools, they identify the administrators as the leaders but rarely identify themselves or their colleagues (LeBlanc & Shelton, 1997).

Most teachers readily agree that they are indeed leaders when the term teacher leadership is defined and described for them. When this realization occurs, which many teachers describe as an epiphany, it is often a pivotal moment in a teacher's professional development because it has the potential to empower the efficacy of the teacher. It is believed that as more teachers begin to see themselves as leaders, the result will be a more empowered profession.

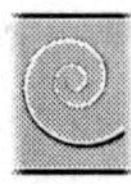

WHY IS TEACHER LEADERSHIP IMPORTANT?

Teachers are the backbone of the school. Teachers represent the majority of adults present in a school. Teachers are a rich resource for schools that should be utilized more because they are agents of change simply by making a difference in the classroom (Darling-Hammond & Sykes, 2003). Teachers are experts in their field, especially in the area of what methods work in practice. It is important for teachers to be able to recognize and acknowledge the many leadership roles that they fulfill. Being labeled and recognized as a leader will hopefully empower teachers to step forward and have a more active voice and role in the field of education and, more specifically, in the teaching profession.

There are many times and opportunities teachers should and need to address educational issues. Too often teachers' input is overlooked, and it seems that important decisions concerning education are made by everyone except those who actually teach. Teachers need to realize that it is important to be more assertive in contributing to discussions and decisions that are being made in the development of better teaching practices. When this occurs, Teacher Leadership allows a "continuous inquiry into practice" (Boles & Troen, 1994, p. 24) which, in many cases, moves teachers away from a narrow classroom perspective. Teacher-Leaders frequently implement action research in their classrooms as an area of personal professional growth (Johnson & Hynes, 1997).

Teachers need to learn the fundamental principles of leadership. Teachers are prepared to teach students but often have little or no training and instruction in how to be effective leaders (Boles & Troen, 1994; Carter & Powell, 1992; Riddle, 1992; Weiss, Cambone, & Wyeth, 1992). As teachers assume more leadership roles, they are expected to know how to perform the many and various mechanics of leadership, such as leading a meeting or making a professional presentation. When teachers are placed in these situations without adequate preparation they can be, and often are, stressful and unsuccessful events for the teachers (Wilson, 1993). As a matter of fact, if teachers have an unsuccessful or unpleasant experience leading outside the classroom, many will withdraw and never allow themselves to be placed in those leadership positions again. However, teachers who have been properly prepared as leaders report feeling more confident, finding they are competent in the performance of duties, and verifying their own personal progress and self-confidence (Lewandowski, 1995). In short, teachers need to learn how to lead successfully in various roles (O'Hair & O'Dell, 1995; Pellicer & Anderson, 1995).

WHO ARE TEACHER-LEADERS?

Teacher-Leaders are teachers who are passionate about teaching and effective in the classroom. Teacher-Leaders are teachers who still get excited about teaching and are always seeking new ideas about new approaches to teaching. Leaders are "proactive people who see the future as presenting opportunities to create something better than the present system . . . (who) see change as an opportunity to grow and to prosper . . . (and) continually ask, 'How can we improve this?'" (Lynch, 1993, p. 7). When these teachers are successful in their classroom, they are eager to share with others the key elements of their success and to help their colleagues to duplicate that success. Also, Teacher-Leaders are most curious and "develop habits of inquiry along with mindsets of continuous growth and learning so that they are always seeking new ideas inside and outside their own setting (Johnson & Hynes, 1997, p. 108). There is a freshness that surrounds Teacher-Leaders because they never become stale or stagnant with their teaching nor tire of working with others.

Teacher-Leaders are the teachers toward whom other teachers gravitate. Mooney (1994) found that teachers described Teacher-Leaders as hard-working, involved with innovation, motivating students, and available to other teachers. Their enthusiasm about teaching and learning is highly contagious and they love helping others be successful. Teachers who collaborate with their colleagues are effective in influencing others without the official titles that carry power of a position (Strodl, 1992; Whitaker, 1995). Teachers know the colleagues to turn to when they need help or when things need to get done. Teacher-Leaders serve a critical role in mentoring not only beginning teachers but those who are teaching a different subject area, as well as experienced teachers who are new to the school (Paulu & Winters, 1998). In addition, Teacher-Leaders provide support and encouragement when needed and, in many cases, a willingness to listen. In addition, Teacher-Leaders are often a lot of fun to be around!

Administrators can often identify, quickly and accurately, which of their faculty members are leaders. As a matter of fact, administrators will seek out Teacher-Leaders because these teachers are trustworthy, conscientious, and have a positive effect on their colleagues. Effective Teacher-Leaders are the teachers that administrators will turn to when they need assistance. Donaldson (2000) suggests that principals should share their leadership with teachers because it will benefit everyone. It is important that all teachers become effective leaders at various levels within the profession by creating a stronger profession with many benefits.

WHAT IS THE PRIMARY PURPOSE OF TEACHER-LEADERS?

The primary purpose of Teacher-Leaders is to serve and improve the teaching profession. Teacher Leadership holds the potential for significant school change and this is the primary reason for expending energy to promote Teacher Leadership (Katzenmeyer & Moller, 2001). It is important that Teacher-Leaders are curious, informed, articulate, and willing to address the educational issues that will affect the classroom—issues that are being debated and discussed in the community and society. Teacher-Leaders are important facilitators of positive change for continual school improvement; when teachers "take leadership matters of instruction and school organization, authentic change happens" (Miller & O'Shea, 1996, p. 179).

Teacher-Leaders are needed to promote the teaching profession. In other professions, the practitioners are often the primary voices that impact their own profession. The same should be true for teachers! Teacher-Leaders serve the profession by seeking more effective ways to accomplish relevant and important goals, whether in the classroom or at the state, national, or even international level.

How Can You Identify Teacher-Leaders in Your School?

Teacher-Leaders are positive and enthusiastic about teaching. They believe in the efficacy of teaching and are motivated by the success of their students. Teacher-Leaders are also lifelong learners and opportunity seekers. Teacher-Leaders possess many positive characteristics that enable them to be successful in influencing others in many positive ways. One personality characteristic that easily defines a Teacher-Leader is unselfishness: Teacher-Leaders are unselfish with their time, resources, and knowledge. They are also hardworking individuals who are not satisfied with the status quo. They want the best, even if it means additional work or effort on their part. Teacher-Leaders are courageous and dignified, and they believe in themselves as well as the good of humanity.

What Are Teacher Leadership Roles in Your School?

Teacher-Leaders have many leadership roles within their school, some of which are formal whereas others are informal. Formal roles include mentor, grade chair, or chairperson of various committees. Informal roles include helping new teachers (but not in the formal mentor role) or organizing and attending various social functions of the school, including Parent-Teacher Association events. Regardless, whether the roles are formal or informal, all teacher leadership roles are important and necessary for schools to function smoothly and effectively.

How Are Teacher-Leaders Selected to Fill These Roles?

Often Teacher-Leaders will simply emerge through their willingness to step forward, to serve, and to become known as important role models within the faculty. Sometimes Teacher-Leaders are selected by their peers. Colleagues become aware of those who have what it takes to be influential and effective in reaching worthy goals and objectives. Often, administrators will select members of their faculty to serve in various leadership roles.

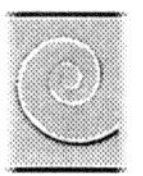

WHAT ARE THE QUALITIES AND CHARACTERISTICS NECESSARY FOR TEACHER LEADERSHIP?

First of all, Teacher-Leaders have a sense of purpose and direction. It is important that Teacher-Leaders have a Personal Professional Statement. Teacher-Leaders must have a clear definition of who they are and what they believe. They must also have a Personal Professional Vision because they are goal-oriented individuals.

Specifically, Teacher-Leaders must have clearly defined goals and objectives. Positive influence, positive direction, and positive change are often the desired outcomes of Teacher Leadership. Teacher-Leaders are ultimately driven by their actions in the classroom, which in turn positively affect their students. Teacher-Leaders never forget that learning and mastery of content by the students are their primary goals.

SUMMARY

Teacher-Leaders are important and their roles in leadership should be more distinctly recognized by the educational profession and society. Leadership is an inherent role of teaching and teachers need to address and learn the essential skills of leadership. As teachers assume more leadership roles beyond the classroom, they need to possess and apply basic leadership skills to be effective. Too often, teachers do not define themselves as leaders; they do not realize the need to learn the necessary leadership skills.

CASE STUDIES

Case 1: Mrs. Jones has been teaching fifth grade at Longmeadow Elementary School for seventeen years. Mrs. Jones is constantly seeking new ideas and innovative teaching approaches to ensure that her students have the best possible instruction. Her students take standardized tests at the end of the year and Mrs. Jones realizes that she is held accountable for their achievement. Mrs. Jones is a hardworking teacher who motivates her students to succeed, accommodates the diversity of learning styles among her students, and is available for other teachers, who gravitate to her for help and advice. The principal of Longmeadow Elementary School often asks for Mrs. Jones' opinions and aid in administrative matters, including projects, parental situations, and suggestions to improve the school environment. Is Mrs. Jones a leader? If so, what attributes make her a leader?

Case 2: Mrs. Rathburne has been teaching for thirty years at the second-grade level at Parkview Elementary School. Mrs. Rathburne teaches to the average learner and lets the reading specialist deal with the students who are struggling with reading. Any time Mrs. Rathburne receives a notice of a workshop in her mail-

Continued

box, she simply throws it away in the garbage. After all, she has been teaching for thirty years, what more does she need to know? Mrs. Rathburne clocks in at 8:00 a.m. and checks out at 3:15 p.m. and is available only at mandatory school functions, such as open house, the holiday play, and scheduled teacher-parent conferences. Mrs. Rathburne's filing cabinets are overflowing with lessons and teaching materials that she has accumulated over the years; she figures she does not need any current material because everything she needs is located in her files. Is Mrs. Rathburne a leader? If so, what attributes make her a leader?

ACTIVITIES

Activity 1: Discovering Your Roles and Values. Here is an activity that will help you to clarify your professional roles and values.

1. On a sheet of paper, write your professional roles. If you are a second-grade teacher, your list might include the following: colleague, mentor, graduate student, member of school improvement committee, grade level chair. With a little bit of reflection, you will likely generate a list of many professional roles. However, the number of professional roles that you have will depend on where you are in your career. A first-year teacher will have a different list than a fourteen-year veteran! The point of this first step is to list the many "hats" that you wear as a professional.

2. Now, take those roles you have identified and break them down into sub-roles. With careful thought, for example, you will realize that the role of a colleague has a number of sub-roles, including friend, supporter, cheerleader, and so on. As you list these roles and sub-roles, you will notice that you are actually addressing the subject of your values. For example, if you listed "nurturer" as a sub-role under the role of mentor, that says something about the way you view and value the role of mentor. It also says something about your priorities and your decisions to optimize your time investments.

3. Keep at it. Write down as many roles as you can think of, then under each one list the sub-roles pertaining to that role. You will find that many of these sub-roles tend to overlap. For example, the sub-role of friend is appropriate for the roles of cheerleader, neighbor, teacher, etc.

4. The next step is to consider each sub-role and the character traits that you feel appropriately support the sub-role. Under the sub-role of friend, you might list such characteristics as loyalty, reliability, patience, and so forth.

5. Through all of this, you are clarifying your values. You are not creating your values, you are discovering and possibly rediscovering them. This is an important process, for truly effective leaders base their decisions and responses on their values because they are value-based and principle-centered. Clarifying

our core values and principles enables us to live our lives more effectively. When we do not define who we are and what we believe, we are more likely to make decisions and respond to situations and circumstances that are not consistent with our values and principles. When that happens, we go through life in the reactive mode. Effective leaders are proactive, not reactive!

Activity 2: Developing your written Personal Professional Mission Statement.

Many of us might believe that we do not need a written document to guide our professional career. We believe that we already know what we want to accomplish in our professional life. However, research shows that when people patiently and diligently work through the process of clarifying their roles and values and develop a Personal Professional Mission Statement, they create focus and balance within their professional life. To develop your written Personal Professional Mission Statement, you need to remember the following steps. First, a written Personal Professional Mission Statement is an ever-evolving document that should be frequently referred to and revised when necessary. Thus, your first attempt should have "First Draft" clearly stated at the top. Second, drafting a Personal Professional Mission Statement requires careful thought, reflection, and consideration.

Most well-written Personal Professional Mission Statements contain two basic elements: a declaration of what you want to do, and a declaration of what you want to be. The following will likely occur during the development of your Personal Professional Mission Statement:

1. You will be compelled to think deeply and strategically about your professional life. The process expands your perspective and causes you to examine your deepest thoughts. It challenges you to resolve the inevitable conflicts between the "wants" and the "shoulds" in your professional life, enabling you to identify and clarify the purpose of your professional life and the beliefs and values that are important to you.

2. The very act of writing it all down is often therapeutic and clarifying in and of itself. Undergoing the discipline of succinctly expressing such important thoughts can help you to better understand what you value and believe.

3. The act of writing the document imprints your values and purposes firmly in your mind, where they become impressions cemented within your identity rather than just random ideas that are briefly pondered and then set aside.

4. The document provides a tangible tool that provides hope, vision, and strategic plans for your professional life. Investing in a Personal Professional Mission Statement pays huge personal effectiveness dividends. Remember, do not take shortcuts! Do not expect to draft a meaningful mission statement in a single sitting. It is a process, not an event. A Personal Professional Mission Statement evolves over time by forcing you to think deeply, critically, and strategically about your professional life. The process expands your perspective and causes you to critically examine your deepest thoughts, values, and beliefs. As previously stated, it challenges you to resolve the inevitable conflicts between the "wants" and the "shoulds" in your professional life, and enables you to identify and clarify the purpose of your professional life as well as the values and beliefs that are most important to you.

Activity 3: Having a Plan of Action:

After writing your Personal Professional Mission Statement, you will have a road map to guide your professional career. A teacher will use the Mission Statement to deliberately plan how to expend time and resources. At the beginning of each week, you should identify and write two or three well-defined goals that you would like to accomplish during the week or other specific time period. These specific goals will help you to generate good intentions into specific actions that will produce results.

Developing well-defined goals and objectives creates a personal roadmap for your future personal and professional life. Goals and objectives provide direction and traction, make your overall vision attainable, provide measures for success, clarify all roles, and give people something to reach for. However, make sure that your goals are SMART Goals! SMART Goals consist of the following: S = specific, M = measurable, A = attainable, R = relevant, T = time-bound.

DISCUSSION QUESTIONS

1. How do teachers become leaders?
2. What are some of the characteristics of Teacher-Leaders?
3. Should Teacher Leadership be encouraged and promoted? Why or why not?
4. Where and how do teachers learn Teacher Leadership skills? Are there better ways to develop such skills?

REFERENCES

Boles, K., & Troen, V. (1994, April). *Teacher leadership in a professional development school.* Paper presented at the annual meeting of the American Educational Research Association, New Orleans.

Carter, M., & Powell, D. (1992). Teacher leaders as staff developers. *Journal of Staff Development, 13*(1), 8–12.

Clemson-Ingram, R., & Fessler, R. (1997). Innovative programs for Teacher Leadership. *Action in Teacher Education, 19*(3), 95–106.

Darling-Hammond, L., & Sykes, G. (2003). Wanted: A national teacher supply policy for education: The right way to meet the “highly qualified teacher” challenge. *Educational Policy Analysis Archives, II* (33), 1–56.

Donaldson, G. A. (2000). *Cultivating leadership in schools: Connecting people, purpose, and practice.* New York: Teachers College Press.

Forster, E. M. (1997). Teacher Leadership: Professional right and responsibility. *Action in Teacher Education, 19*(3), 82–94.

Gardner, J. W. (1989). *On leadership.* New York: Free Press.

Johnson, J., & Hynes, M. C. (1997). Teacher/learning/leading: Synonyms for change. *Action in Teacher Education, 19*(3), 107–119.

Katzenmeyer, M., & Moller, G. (2001). *Awakening the sleeping giant: Helping teachers develop as leaders.* Thousand Oaks, CA: Corwin.

Keedy, T., & Finch, A. (1994). Examining teacher principal empowerment: An analysis of power. *Journal of Research and Development in Education 27,*162–173.

LeBlanc, P. R., & Shelton, M. M. (1997). Teacher Leadership: The need of teachers. *Action in Teacher Education, 19*(3), 32–48.

Lewandowski, A. (1995). *Leadership development for teachers: 1995 evaluation.* Tampa: West Central Educational Leadership Network.

Lynch, R. (1993). *LEAD!* San Fransico: Jossey-Bass.

Miller, L., & O'Shea, C. (1996). School-university partnership: Getting broader, getting deeper. In M. W. McLaughlin & I. Oberman (Eds.), *Teacher learning: New policies, new practices* (pp. 161–181). New York: Teachers College Press.

Mooney, T. (1994). *Teachers as leaders: Hope for the future.* Washington, D.C.: ERIC (ERIC Document Reproduction Service No. ED 380–407).

O'Hair, M. J., & Odell, S. J. (1995). *Educating teachers for leadership and change.* Thousand Oaks, CA: Corwin.

O'Hair, M. J., & Reitzug, U. C. (1997). Teacher Leadership: In what ways? For what purpose? *Action in Teacher Education, 19*(3), 65–76.

Paulu, N., & Winters, K. (Eds.). (1998). *Teachers leading the way: Voices from the National Teacher Forum* (Report No. EDD00001). Washington, D.C.: Department of Education. (ERIC Document Reproduction Service No. ED 419 778).

Pellicer, L., & Anderson, L. (1995). *A Handbook for Teacher Leaders.* Newbury, CA: Corwin.

Riddle, F. (1992*).* Case Studies of Teachers as Leaders and Change Agents in School Improvement and Restructuring. Ann Arbor: University microfilms.

Sirotnik, K., & Kimball, K. (1995, March). *Preparing educators for leadership: In praise of experience.* Paper presented at the annual meeting of the American Educational Research Association, San Francisco.

Stone, M., Horejs, J., & Lomas, A. (1997). Commonalities and differences in teacher leadership at the elementary, middle, and high school level. *Action in Teacher Education, 19*(3), 107–119.

Strodl, P. (1992, March). *A model of teacher leadership.* Paper presented at the annual meeting of the Eastern Educational Research Association, Hilton Head, SC.

Weiss, C. H., Cambone, J., & Wyeth, A. (1992). Trouble in paradise: Teacher conflicts in shared decision making. *Educational Administration Quarterly, 28,* 350–367.

Whitaker, T. (1995). Informal teacher leadership—The key to successful change in middle level schools. *NAASP Bulletin, 79*(567), 76–81.

Wilson, M. (1993). The search for Teacher-Leaders. *Educational Leadership, 50*(6), 24–27.

Chapter 2

Teachers Are Designers

This chapter will introduce the concept of Teacher-Designer and how it can be applied in the school setting and within the field of education. The concept of Teacher-Designer is another critical piece of the theoretical framework of Teacher-Leader/Designer. This chapter will first define the concept of Teacher-Designer and describe theoretical underpinnings of this concept. We describe how to identify characteristics of an effective Teacher-Designer, discuss the importance of a Teacher-Designer perspective, and define specific Teacher-Designer roles within a school setting. At the end of this chapter, readers should be able to define the term Teacher-Designer and identify the origins of this concept, identify the characteristics of a Teacher-Designer, list specific roles of a Teacher-Designer within a school setting, and describe the potential and impact of Teacher-Designers in the schools.

After reading this chapter, you will be able to:

1. Define Teacher-Designer.
2. Identify the origins of the Teacher-Designer concept.
3. Describe why Teacher-Designers are important.
4. Identify who Teacher-Designers are in a school setting.
5. Describe the primary purpose of Teacher-Designers.
6. List the characteristics of Teacher-Designers.
7. Identify some of the main roles of Teacher-Designers.
8. Describe the desired outcomes of becoming a Teacher-Designer.
9. Identify Teacher-Designer skills and characteristics in yourself and others.

TEACHER-DESIGNER—WHAT IS IT?

Whereas a Teacher-Leader is an established concept as documented in the previously cited literature (see chapter 1), the Teacher-Designer concept has not been as extensively established. Building on the theoretical foundation of the Teacher-Leader, the Teacher-Designer also is a natural consequence of being an effective and proactive teacher. A designer conceives and creates to achieve certain outcomes. In the case of teachers, the desired outcomes are cognitive achievement, as well as the social-emotional growth of their students. The activities of a Teacher-Designer range from how to arrange the classroom to how to teach curricular goals and objectives. Effective and proactive teachers are constantly seeking and designing new approaches to teaching. Increasingly, teachers are being asked to implement technology into the curriculum (e.g., North Carolina Dept. of Public Instruction, 2003). To facilitate this implementation, we propose that teachers adopt a Teacher-Designer perspective. It is essential for teachers to view themselves as *Designers*. By assuming this perspective, we believe teachers will become effective technology users in their classrooms and within their schools.

TEACHER-DESIGNER—WHERE DID IT COME FROM?

As with Teacher-Leaders, we believe that Teachers-Designers have always existed in the schools. We base this belief on the simple fact that teachers naturally design instruction. Yes, teachers naturally are designers. For example, at the end of a school year, a principal approached a fourth-grade teacher and told him that he would be switched over to teaching the first grade the following year. During his summer break, this teacher investigated the specific first-grade goals from the state's standard course of study, reviewed his first-grade colleagues' existing lesson plans, and examined his school district's first-grade textbook. By the beginning of the following school year, this teacher was prepared to teach the first three units in all of the core areas. He also had a working knowledge in all of the first-grade curriculum units. It is obvious that this teacher will likely be a successful first-grade teacher.

This teacher's preparation is quite common among first-year teachers or teachers who are switching over to teaching a new grade. In fact, *all* teachers prepare or design their lessons. That is, teachers naturally are designers of instructional materials. Not only is design found in instructional settings, it is found in several disciplines, including human–computer interface design and engineering. Below, we describe how design is implemented in these two disciplines and the relationship between the overall nature of design and a Teacher-Designer.

One of the tenets of a Teacher-Designer is found in the human–computer interface design discipline. This design theory affirms the direct involvement of users in the decision-making process. Users' needs must be *integral* in the design of software applications; these needs should *dominate* the designs of the application's interface and other corresponding parts (Norman, 1986). Donald Norman (1988, 1998), who originally coined the term *human-centered design*, advocates that software developers must acknowledge, respect, and comprehend the needs of humans (e.g., users, learners, students) when they create their products. According to Norman, we need to take into account the cognitive processes involved and cognitive limitations of our users, as well as other factors (e.g., affective domain). This philosophy sets up an alternative relationship between a software developer and their audience. These developers must serve their users' needs, while users take on a more proactive role in the development of technological products. This new relationship affects teachers, who continually develop and implement effective instructional interventions in their respective classrooms, and enables teachers to become Teacher-Designers in their respective classrooms.

Another contributing factor of a Teacher-Designer is found in the engineering literature and in Henry Petroski's writings (e.g., Petroski, 1985; 1996). Petroski associates engineering and engineers with the world of design and designers. We believe that teachers have a similar relationship with Petroski's design ideas and philosophy. The design skills involved with building bridges, satellites, or next-generation computers are similar to the skills involved with developing effective instructional lessons. Design is "making something that has not existed before . . ." (Petroski, 1985).

Petroski noted the following principles that are associated with design. He claimed that design essentially is a form of proposing specific hypotheses. That is, to develop a new design, a designer essentially proposes a new hypothesis relative to the old design. For example, car engineers design a new automobile model partially based upon an earlier model, but also design new features based upon a particular hypothesis (e.g., front-wheel drive will perform better than rear-wheel drive). An educational hypothesis might be a ninth-grade lesson plan on branches of government that is partially based upon an earlier lesson plan, but which also relies on specific hypotheses (e.g., students will learn more effectively by role playing each of the major roles of the three branches of government).

In addition to proposing these hypotheses, Petroski affirmed that designers also try to anticipate failure and design their products to avoid potential obstacles. In fact, teachers may anticipate potential problems with a particular content area based upon earlier lessons and adjust their redesigned lesson accordingly. This is what Petroski labeled as a continual revision process between the design of a product, the evaluation of a product, and the pending revision of a product. Petroski documented this design and revision process with a variety of products, including the design of paperclips (Petroski, 1996), pencils (Petroski, 1990), zippers (Petroski, 1996), and other items.

Petroski observed, "Products of engineering are all around us." (Petroski, 1996, p. 1). As educators, we also claim that products of instruction are all around us. The instructional quality of one's community is dependent on the design efforts of its teachers. Individuals who design instruction, such as Teacher-Designers, essentially rely on applying what Reigeluth (1983) labeled as a prescriptive science. That is, teachers "prescribe" a particular lesson plan based upon known and effective educational principles. Several proponents (e.g., Simon, 1996) urged educators to apply social science principles in a manner similar to how doctors prescribe a treatment based upon scientific principles (e.g., diagnosis). This is what John Dewey (1997) referred to as a "linking science" between learning theory and educational practice. The result of a Teacher-Designers' ability to "link" and prescribe an effective instructional solution is the product of one's instruction. The ultimate outcome of this product is an educated society.

As stated earlier, teachers are naturally Teacher-Designers. Teachers continually assess learners' feedback about a particular lesson. Teachers are always proposing a new "hypothesis" about how to redesign the next instructional unit and are in a continual revision process. To participate in this process, Teacher-Designers "prescribe" instructional solutions by "linking" educational principles. Understanding the multiple sources of this existing literature elevates the importance of a Teacher-Designer and solidifies the role of the Teacher-Designer.

WHO ARE TEACHER-DESIGNERS?

Like Teacher-Leaders, Teacher-Designers are teachers who are passionate about teaching and who are effective in the classroom. Their unwavering enthusiasm about teaching naturally conjures the design abilities and competencies of Teacher-Designers. With this passion for teaching, teachers will want to continually revise their respective lessons, constantly evaluate learners' feedback about their instruction, and prescribe effective learning solutions based upon instructionally sound principles. Also, teachers who strive for excellence in their respective classrooms will rely heavily on their design skills. That is, to create an effective learning environment, teachers must consciously and continually design quality lessons. In fact, one of the main set of design tools utilized by teachers comes from the domain of instructional technology and media tools. We elaborate on developing these effective technology skills of a Teacher-Leader/Designer in chapter 6.

WHAT ARE THE COMMON CHARACTERISTICS OF A TEACHER-DESIGNER?

There are several instances where teachers can assert their leadership skills (e.g., chairing a meeting, mentoring a first-year teacher), but Teacher-Designer skills are not as evident. Often only extraordinary design or technology skills of respective teachers are noticed. Thus, characteristics of Teacher-Designers are not apparent. However, we believe that a Teacher-Designer would inherently affect these similar events at a school. A teacher who proactively adheres to Teacher-Designer principles would communicate to other teachers and staff members a tacit message of being a Teacher-Designer. For instance, in a mentoring session, a teacher mentor and a novice teacher might discuss successful and unsuccessful teaching methods. A teacher mentor, who endorses a Teacher-Designer viewpoint, would overtly and tacitly profess a Teacher-Designer message to the novice teacher. Similarly, a Teacher-Designer, who is chairing a school improvement plan meeting would overtly and tacitly profess a Teacher-Designer message and directly influence the outcome of this plan. A Teacher-Designer is not limited exclusively to situations involving teaching practices and technology, but can be involved in decisions affecting the entire school.

WHAT ARE POSSIBLE TEACHER-DESIGNER ROLES IN YOUR SCHOOL?

Before we provide examples of possible Teacher-Designer roles in the classroom, we want to briefly summarize three alternative perspectives about technology (Sugar, 2002). These three perspectives are the foundation of the Teacher-Designer concept and provide further insight into this initiative. As shown in Figure 2.1, there are three technology perspectives: *Assertive technology, Adaptive technology,* and *Compelling technology.* You will note that each technology perspective has three corresponding mottos, the intent of which is to illustrate the respective technology perspective.

The intention of these perspectives is to "provide possible solutions to intangible obstacles to technology integration (e.g., lack of confidence)" and to "influence educators' beliefs toward technology integration" (Sugar, 2002, p. 12). *Assertive technology* encourages and acknowledges teachers' proactive role in technology use and decision making. *Adaptive technology* requires technology to adapt to teachers' needs, rather than teachers adapting to technology. *Compelling technology* demands technology to facilitate creativity and to solve teachers' specific problems.

Assertive Technology
- It is not your fault; it is the designers' fault.
- I can use "old" technology, as long as it is effective for my students.
- I am a designer of technology, rather than a user of technology.

Adaptive Technology
- Technology will *conform* to my proposed needs, not the designer's needs.
- It is fine to make "errors" with technology; technology will adapt to my mistakes.
- Technology is designed and used to solve *my* problems.

Compelling Technology
- Effective technology is appropriate and practical.
- The *sole* purpose of technology is to help me be more creative.
- The more active user I am, the more effective the technology will be.

Figure 2.1 Alternative Technology Perspectives and Corresponding Mottos (adapted from Sugar, 2002)

HOW TO BECOME A TEACHER-DESIGNER IN THE CLASSROOM

Our Teacher-Designer concept is composed primarily of the first two technology perspectives, *Assertive technology* and *Adaptive technology*. That is, to become Teacher-Designers, teachers must *assert* their proactive role in technology decision making and make demands that technology be *adaptive* to their needs. A Teacher-Designer still expects technology to be compelling, but the *Compelling technology* perspective mostly lies outside the realm of a Teacher-Designer.

Below we discuss the roles that Assertive technology and Adaptive technology take in the formation of a Teacher-Designer in the classroom.

ASSERTIVE TECHNOLOGY

Each of the corresponding mottos of Assertive technology elevates the role of teachers with regards to technology and points to the fact that teachers are in control of the use of technology in their classroom. Adopting an Assertive technology perspective enables teachers to "assert" and affirm their expertise as designers. The motto "old technology is fine to use, as long it is effective" gives teachers the opportunity and authority to say "no" to integrating new technologies in their classroom, if these new technologies are not effective in the teacher's particular classroom. We trust that teachers will make the correct design decision in selecting the appropriate technology for their classrooms, and also be continually seeking alternative and more effective ways of teaching their students. We believe that the motto "I am a designer of technology, rather than a user of technology" states the obvious. Because teachers are naturally designers, they continually design and revise their lessons to meet their students' learning needs. An Assertive technology perspective reaffirms this expertise and persuades teachers to proactively utilize technology and relevant materials in their classroom.

When should one use an Assertive technology perspective? Given the choice of selecting and adopting a "new" technology (e.g., software application) in the classroom, teachers need to decide whether this particular technology suits the particular context of their classroom. Teachers who exhibit an Assertive technology perspective should not rely solely on outside opinions, but teachers can *assert* their professional opinion on whether there is an effective match. The potential adoption of an online grade book is a good example. Because teachers who adopt an Assertive technology perspective are "designers of technology" rather than "users of technology" (see Figure 2.1), they can take a proactive stance and decide whether an online grade book makes sense in their particular classroom. She may decide that it doesn't fit due to hardware or software constraints or other factors. However, we are not advocating that Assertive technology teachers become "laggards" (Rogers, 2003) and never adopt new technologies. As shown in Figure 2.1, an Assertive technology perspective prescribes that "'old' technology is fine" to use, but it has a stipulation: Teachers must determine that the technology they are using is *effective* with their particular group of students.

ADAPTIVE TECHNOLOGY

As stated in Sugar (2002, p. 15), this particular perspective has its roots in Donald Norman's (1993) human-centered motto for the twenty-first century. As opposed to the 1933 Chicago World's Fair motto *"Science Finds, Industry Applies, Man Conforms,"* Norman proposes a twenty-first century human-centered motto *"People Propose, Science Studies, Technology Conforms."* Put into context, technology must conform or *adapt* to teachers' needs. Too often, teachers (and others) who do not subscribe to the Adaptive technology perspective believe that they must adapt to a particular technology. The authors, as well as others (e.g., Donald Norman), believe that this belief is erroneous and instead advocate that technology should adapt to teachers' needs. Both mottos, "Technology will *conform* to my proposed needs, not designer's needs" and "It is fine to make 'errors' with technology; technology will adapt to my mistakes," reflect this emphasis. Like the Assertive technology perspective, the Adaptive technology perspective invites, encourages, and allows teachers to be proactive in their decisions regarding technology. This proactive nature is encapsulated in our Teacher-Designer perspective.

Again, how can teachers apply the Adaptive technology perspective? Let's revisit the online grade book example. While reviewing a new technology, such as an online grade book, teachers can use the three Adaptive technology mottos (see Figure 2.1) as an evaluation checklist, and ask themselves the following questions. Does this online grade book *conform* or fulfill my classroom needs? Can this online grade book *adapt* to my mistakes and does it have a "forgiving" interface? Most important, can this online grade book *solve* my current problem? If a teacher responds positively to these three questions, there is strong evidence for adopting this new technology. Conversely, if a majority of these responses are negative, then a teacher has proof for *not* adopting this new technology.

WHY IS A TEACHER-DESIGNER IMPORTANT?

We are quite confident that after reading this chapter you will agree that teachers are indeed designers. In fact, if teachers did not design their respective lessons, a major deficit in providing quality instruction to students would exist. Teachers who are not designers, will simply not survive as successful teachers. Consequently, a Teacher-Designer perspective is essential for those teachers who are striving to succeed in their profession and for the continual development of quality instruction.

SUMMARY

Teacher-Designers are important and teachers' roles as designers should be recognized more distinctly by the educational profession and society in general. Like leadership skills, design skills are an inherent role of teaching, and essential design skills need to be addressed and learned by teachers. To remain effective and successful, teachers need to continually apply their design skills in creating their lessons and educational experiences for their students. Just as teachers often fail to recognize their inherent leadership skills, they usually do not define themselves as designers. It is revitalizing to assume that this Teacher-Designer perspective will enhance one's role as a teacher.

CASE STUDIES

Case 1: Mr. Gene Adams has been a sixth-grade teacher at Michael J. Haynes Middle School for fifteen years. Previously, he was a fifth-grade teacher at an elementary in the same school district. Haynes Middle School teachers consider Mr. Adams to be a maverick. He is continually seeking new ways to instruct his students with an assortment of new technologies, and he also attends the school district advanced technology workshops. He even has taught a couple of PowerPoint® workshops during faculty meetings. Mr. Dodd, the assistant principal, always recommends that new teachers seek Mr. Adams' advice. He encourages these first-year and second-year teachers to "go talk to Gene and find out what he knows about technology." Teachers often hear Haynes Middle School students talk about the fun things that happen in Mr. Adams' class. Is Mr. Adams a Teacher-Designer? If so, what attributes make him a Teacher-Designer?

Case 2: Ms. Cugelson has been teaching for twenty-six years as a foreign language teacher at Van Oaks High School. Ms. Cugelson became department chair nine years ago. For the first six years of her career, she taught Latin and Spanish. Now she mainly teaches beginning and advanced Spanish, and occasionally teaches an Italian class for her school district and the neighboring school district. As the chair of the Foreign Language department, she must provide leadership on how to implement the state's revised standards for the foreign language curriculum. She also mentors younger teachers on how best to teach students a second language. She encourages students to practice their Spanish and Italian by posing certain situations (e.g., ordering food from a menu, giving directions to a tourist, making phone calls). Is Ms. Cugelson a Teacher-Designer? If so, what attributes makes her a Teacher-Designer?

ACTIVITIES

Activity 1: Discovering Your Own Teacher-Designer Skills. Reflect on your role as a Teacher-Designer. List activities that you perform as a Teacher-Designer. Develop a plan of action in developing additional Teacher-Designer skills.

Activity 2: Interview three teachers and find out what activities they perform as a Teacher-Designer. Interview your principal or assistant principal about the activities that they perform as a Teacher-Designer.

Activity 3: As described in this chapter, the concept of Teacher-Designer is composed of several design theories. Reflect upon these theories and principles and how you could potentially implement them in your own teaching. Specifically, how do you incorporate your students' feedback into your own instruction? Do you continually revise and propose hypotheses about your lesson plans? If so, how? How do you "prescribe" instructional solutions based upon educational principles?

DISCUSSION QUESTIONS

1. How do teachers become designers?
2. Summarize and categorize the characteristics of Teacher-Designers that you have found in your school.
3. Where and how do teachers learn Teacher-Designer skills? What are some ways to learn these skills? Propose possible ways to become a more effective Teacher-Designer?

REFERENCES

Dewey, J. (1997). *How We Think.* Mineola, NY: Dover.

Norman, D. (1986). Cognitive engineering. In D. Norman and S. Draper (Eds.), *User centered system design: New perspectives on human-computer interaction* (pp. 31–61). Hillsdale, NJ: L. Erlbaum.

Norman, D. (1988). *The Psychology of Everyday Things.* New York: Basic Books.

Norman, D. (1993). *Things That Make Us Smart: Defending Human Attributes in the Age of the Machine.* Reading, MA: Addison-Wesley.

Norman, D. (1998). *Invisible Computer: Why Good Products Can Fail, the Personal Computer is So Complex and Information Appliances Are the Solution.* Cambridge, MA: MIT.

North Carolina Dept. of Public Instruction. (2003). *IMPACT model grant request for proposals.* Retrieved July 15, 2004, from http://tps.dpi.state.nc.us/eett/eett/IMPACTgrantfinal.html.

Petroski, H. (1985). *To Engineer is Human: The Role of Failure in Successful Design.* New York: St. Martin's.

Petroski, H. (1990). *The Pencil: A History of Design and Circumstance.* New York: Knopf.

Petroski, H. (1996). *Invention by Design: How Engineers Get from Thought to Thing.* Cambridge, MA: Harvard University.

Reigeluth, C. M. (1983). *Instructional Design Theories and Models: An Overview of Their Current Status.* Hillsdale, NJ: Erlbaum.

Rogers, E. M. (2003). *Diffusion of Innovations.* (5th ed.). New York: Free Press.

Simon, H. (1996). *The Sciences of the Artificial.* (3rd ed.). Cambridge, MA: MIT.

Sugar, W. (2002). Applying human-centered design to technology integration: Three alternative technology perspectives. *Journal of Computing in Teacher Education, 19*(1), 12–17.

Chapter 3

Teachers Are Leaders and Designers

This chapter will introduce the concept of a Teacher-Leader/Designer and discuss its relationship with a Teacher-Leader and a Teacher-Designer. The importance of this concept in the teaching profession and within the field of education is also addressed. This chapter will define the term Teacher-Leader/Designer and describe the origins of this concept. We also define the assumptions that underlie a Teacher-Leader/Designer and the observable characteristics of a Teacher-Leader/Designer within a school setting. At the end of this chapter, readers should be able to define the term Teacher-Leader/Designer and describe the origins of this concept, identify Teacher-Leader/Designers, identify the specific roles of a Teacher-Leader/Designer within a school setting, and describe the potential and impact of a Teacher-Leader/Designer on schools.

After reading this chapter, you will be able to:

1. Define Teacher-Leader/Designer.
2. Identify where the concept of Teacher-Leader/Designer comes from.
3. Describe why Teacher-Leader/Designers are important.
4. Identify who Teacher-Leader/Designers are in a school setting.
5. Describe the primary purpose of Teacher-Leader/Designers.
6. List the characteristics of Teacher-Leader/Designers.
7. Identify the inherent assumptions of Teacher-Leader/Designers.
8. Identify Teacher-Leader/Designer skills and characteristics in yourself and others.
9. Update a Personal Professional Mission Statement with the addition of Teacher-Leader/Designer skills.

TEACHER-LEADER/DESIGNER—WHAT IS IT?

Now that we have described the Teacher-Leader and Teacher-Designer concepts separately, we would like to address the combination and integration of these two concepts. This combination of Teacher-Leader and Teacher-Designer will be discussed as an integrated, cohesive perspective. Essentially, our proposed Teacher-Leader/Designer conception presents teachers with an alternative mindset in viewing their role as a teacher. It is geared toward teachers' affective domain and how they perceive themselves as a teacher. It invites teachers to take on a proactive role as a teacher. To be an effective teacher, qualities of a Teacher-Leader/Designer need to be consciously and overtly expressed.

Thus, a Teacher-Leader/Designer essentially is a combination of the Teacher-Leader concept with the Teacher-Designer concept. A Teacher-Leader/Designer is not radically different from a Teacher-Leader, but it is a modification of the original Teacher-Leader concept. This modified concept simply acknowledges teachers' unified ability and role as leaders and designers. As a Teacher-Leader/Designer, teachers can be proactive participants in the future direction of their school.

How does a Teacher-Leader/Designer differ from a Teacher-Leader? We assert that a Teacher-Leader/Designer is a modification and an addition to the Teacher-Leader concept rather than a radical alteration. This modified label simply acknowledges teachers' ability and role as a designer in proactively promoting technology in their respective classrooms. A Teacher-Leader/Designer still adheres to the principles of constructivism and democratic leadership where the focus is on leadership acts rather than leadership roles (O'Hair & Reitzug, 1997). Johnson and Hynes' (1997) self-reflective motto "Teachers as Learners, Learners as Leaders" is still evident in a Teacher-Leader/Designer model. Teachers should still ask how they can improve teaching, leadership, and design practices in their classroom, school, and community.

To further illustrate similarities between a Teacher-Leader/Designer and a Teacher-Leader, we address the following qualities of a Teacher-Leader as described by Bishop, Tinley, and Berman (1997), who proposed three elements to promote a Teacher-Leader environment (pp. 78–79). These elements include: establishment of appropriate school culture; recognition of Teacher-Leaders; and inspiring teachers' confidence. All of these three elements are important for a Teacher-Leader/Designer. Principals and superintendents must espouse an appropriate school culture, or a "caring community culture" (O'Hair & Reitzug, 1997). These administrators should implement policies that recognize teachers as designers as well as leaders. Such policies would give teachers a proactive role in making decisions about the use of technology in their respective classrooms and beyond.

Teachers often erroneously believe that administrators are in control of the use of technology in their classrooms and in the schools (Sugar, Crawley, & Fine, 2004). School leaders should follow Bishop, Tinley, and Berman's (1997) lead and establish a culture that recognizes teachers' ability to be a Teacher-Designer. These proposed policies would give teachers the authority to implement an assertive technology perspective within their classrooms.

After this localized control or shared leadership (O'Hair & Reitzug, 1997) is established, we assert that teachers will become more confident with using technology in their new roles as Teachers-Designers. Although there are known external barriers (e.g., limited budgets, insufficient time, limited equipment availability) to implement technology in the classroom, teachers also must overcome affective barriers to the use of technology in the classrooms, or what Ertmer (1999) terms second-order barriers. (For more information on the incentives and obstacles affecting technology use, see Chapter 6.) Establishing a Teacher-Leader/Designer perspective will ultimately overcome these barriers to integrate technology into the classroom, as well as elevating the teacher's role and importance in a school environment.

TEACHER-LEADER/DESIGNER—WHERE DID IT COME FROM?

What exactly is a Teacher-Leader/Designer? Where did this concept originate? We realize that this is a relatively new term for virtually all teachers. However, the foundation of a Teacher-Leader/Designer perspective is connected to two established and interrelated concepts, namely Teacher-Leader and Teacher-Designer. Although the preceding chapters of this book extensively detail these concepts, as well as corresponding philosophy and relevant existing literature, the concepts of Teacher-Leader, Teacher-Designer, and Teacher-Leader/Designer are briefly reviewed below.

Teacher-Leader

For more than ten years, several proponents (e.g., Bolman & Deal, 2002; Katzenmeyer & Moller, 2001) have advocated the Teacher-Leader concept for public school teachers. Effective leadership has always been a vital part of quality teaching. As school reform continues (e.g., No Child Left Behind) to increase at a rapid pace throughout the country, effective Teacher Leadership is more critical than ever. Teachers are naturally leaders, because to lead is to influence, and teachers are always in the position to influence students, colleagues, parents, administrators, and the public. Asserting and acknowledge one's Teacher Leadership skills can be quite influential on the future direction of schools. The key is for teachers to realize and act upon their leadership roles.

Teacher-Designer

Teachers are also designers or Teacher-Designers. A designer is one who conceives, and teachers are constantly conceiving various ideas to act upon in their classroom and beyond. Being a Teacher-Designer is also a natural consequence of being an effective and proactive teacher. A designer conceives and strives to achieve discernible outcomes. In the case of teachers, the desired outcomes range from the cognitive, social-emotional achievement of their students to helping legislators understand various critical needs related to teaching. The basis of this Teacher-Designer concept is established in the human-computer interface design discipline (Norman, 1988), as well as other design theory disciplines (Petroski, 1985).

Teacher-Leader/Designer

A Teacher-Leader/Designer is a combination of the Teacher-Leader concept and the Teacher-Designer concept. A Teacher-Leader/Designer is not radically different from a Teacher-Leader, but it is a modification of the original Teacher-Leader concept. This modified concept simply acknowledges teachers' unified ability and role as leaders and designers. Teacher-Leader/Designers can be proactive participants in the future direction of their school.

WHAT ASSUMPTIONS DO WE HAVE ABOUT TEACHER-LEADER/DESIGNERS?

Similar to Teacher-Leaders, Teacher-Leader/Designers also are teachers who are passionate about teaching and who are effective in the classroom. Similar to Teacher-Designer, Teacher-Leader/Designers actively engage in the design of their students' learning experiences through a variety of means, both technological and nontechnological.

In addition to these common qualities of Teacher-Leaders and Teacher-Designers, we have made certain assumptions about teachers and their ability to positively impact their school's environment. These overarching assumptions are prevalent throughout this book and directly connected to our proposed Teacher-Leader/Designers concept. These assumptions include the following:

- *Teachers have an innate ability to lead and to make an impact.* We are quite confident that motivated teachers who are given the proper environment can impact their students' lives and their respective schools. We are believers in teachers' leadership abilities to transform and affect students through memorable experiences. It may be true that some leadership traits are innate, but it is also true that leadership skills can be learned. This text is designed to instruct teachers on how to apply these leadership skills and activities in their classroom and school.
- *Teachers have an innate ability to design creative instructional solutions.* We believe in teachers' innate expertise in developing lessons that instruct their students about a wide variety of content areas in the cognitive domain, as well as areas in the affective domain. Although teachers may not realize it, they are indeed designers. By adopting a designers' mentality, teachers can change their attitude toward integrating a variety of technological tools into their respective classrooms. This text offers activities and advice on how to adopt a Teacher-Designer mentality.

- *Teachers' ability to lead and their ability to design are interrelated.* Teachers' innate abilities to lead and to design may appear to be two separate entities, but we assert that interrelating these two abilities will create synergy and enliven teachers to be proactive participants in their classroom and school environments. In this book, we describe specific skills, propose activities to promote a Teacher-Leader/Designer perspective, and discuss potential outcomes of interrelating a Teacher-Leader/Designer mentality.

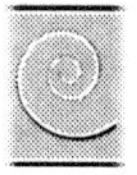

WHAT ARE THE COMMON QUALITIES AND CHARACTERISTICS OF A TEACHER-LEADER, A TEACHER-DESIGNER, AND A TEACHER-LEADER/DESIGNER?

Because a Teacher-Leader/Designer is a combination of a Teacher-Leader and a Teacher-Designer, the qualities and characteristics of a Teacher-Leader and a Teacher-Designer also are found in a Teacher-Leader/Designer. Teacher-Leader/Designers also have a sense of purpose and enthusiasm for teaching. A primary purpose of Teacher-Leader/Designers is to serve students and concentrate on improving schools. Because of this commitment, Teacher-Leader/Designers will also have many leadership roles within their school. These roles will be the same leadership roles that Teacher-Leaders and Teacher-Designers will assume. Like Teacher-Designers, Teacher-Leader/Designers also continually assess their students' feedback about a particular lesson and propose a new "hypothesis" about how to redesign the next instructional unit. Teacher-Leader/Designers are in a continual revision process. To participate in this process, Teacher-Leader/Designers also "prescribe" instructional solutions by "linking" educational principles. Similarly, Teacher-Leader/Designers should have a Personal Professional Mission Statement. In this statement, Teacher-Leader/Designers should clearly define who they are and what they believe in.

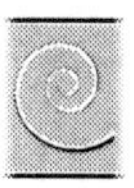

WHY IS A TEACHER-LEADER/DESIGNER IMPORTANT?

One of the primary purposes of this book is to *introduce* the Teacher-Leader/Designer concept to public school teachers. We truly believe that teachers are the "backbone of the school." To effectively manage schools and develop effective learning experiences for students, teachers need to develop a Teacher-Leader/Designer mindset. Thus, becoming or actually recognizing one's Teacher-Leader and Teacher-Designer skills is crucial to becoming a Teacher-Leader/Designer.

There is a distinct advantage to combining one's leadership skills and design skills: Teachers will become active participants in the learning process. By becoming a Teacher-Leader/Designer, teachers will be enthusiastic and dynamic proponents of effective learning in classrooms, schools, and school districts. We are quite confident that Teacher-Leader/Designers will become successful teachers in their respective schools. We encourage you to become an active, enthusiastic, and dynamic Teacher-Leader/Designer at your own school!

SUMMARY

Teacher-Leaders, Teacher-Designers, and Teacher-Leader/Designers are important and their roles as leaders and designers should be recognized more distinctly by the educational profession and society. It is an undeniable fact that leadership skills and design skills are an inherent role of teaching, and essential leadership and design skills need to be addressed and learned by all teachers. Just as they often fail to recognize their inherent leadership skills or design skills, teachers usually do not define themselves as leaders *and* designers. By becoming Teacher-Leader/Designers, teachers will apply their natural leadership and design skills effectively in their respective schools, and will have success in their careers as educators.

CASE STUDIES

Case 1: Mr. Stanley Tewbucky has been teaching fourth grade at Sherman Way Elementary School for three-and-a-half years. Following a sixteen-year military career, he decided to "re-enlist" into a second career as a teacher. After completing a lateral entry program at the local university, Mr. Tewbucky secured a teaching position at Sherman Way. Mr. Tewbucky often relies on his previous military experience to maintain and restore discipline in his classroom. His favorite subjects to teach are science and mathematics. He consults with other fourth-grade teachers to deliver uniform and consistent instructional units. Ms. Dolan-Williams, a first-year principal at Sherman Way, just completed an internal assessment of her teachers and staff. She wants Mr. Tewbucky to take on more of a leadership role next year at Sherman Way. How is Mr. Tewbucky a Teacher-Leader/Designer? What attributes make him a leader? What attributes make him a designer? How can Ms. Dolan-Williams use Mr. Tewbucky's potential Teacher-Leader/Designer skills next year?

Case 2: Ms. Jacobs, principal of Deadwood Intermediate School, was reviewing her teachers' goals for the upcoming school year. Each year, the Mosswood school district requires its teachers to set professional goals. Principals in the district review these goals and develop a plan of action with each teacher in order to meet these goals. Ms. Jacobs noted a unfamiliar term on fifth-grade teacher, Mr. Randy Smith-Blaine's, list of goals. Two of the three goals listed the term, "Teacher-Leader/Designer." Mr. Smith-Blaine's first goal was "Develop my Teacher-Leader/Designer abilities by proposing new curriculum." His second goal stated: "Focus on being a Teacher-Leader/Designer by participating on the School Improvement team." Ms. Jacobs was not familiar with the term Teacher-Leader/Designer, but she recently completed advanced educational leadership training at a local university. How can Mr. Smith-Blaine explain the meaning of his two professional development goals to Ms. Jacobs?

ACTIVITIES

Activity 1: Recognizing Your Teacher-Leader/Designer skills. Here is an activity that will help you clarify your roles as a Teacher-Leader/Designer.

1. Keep a journal of activities that you perform as a teacher during one week. Make sure you keep a detailed listing of your interactions with students, colleagues, administrators, and other school personnel.

2. Categorize these activities as Teacher-Leader activities, Teacher-Designer activities, and Teacher-Leader/Designer activities. You can mark these activities with a "TL", "TD", and "TLD" to represent these three categories.

3. Keep second journal of activities that you perform as a teacher during another week. Make sure you keep a detailed listing of your interactions with students, colleagues, administrators, and other school personnel.

4. Categorize this second list of activities as Teacher-Leader activities, Teacher-Designer activities, and Teacher-Leader/Designer activities. Mark these activities as before.

5. Keep a third journal of activities that you perform as a teacher during one more week. Make sure you keep a detailed listing of your interactions with students, colleagues, administration and other school personnel.

6. Categorize this third list of activities as Teacher-Leader activities, Teacher-Designer activities, and Teacher-Leader/Designer activities. Mark these activities as before.

7. Consult the list describing three weeks of your activities and reflect on how your role as a teacher emulates a Teacher-Leader, Teacher-Designer, and a Teacher-Leader/Designer.

8. Using this list, ask yourself how you can enhance your skills as a Teacher-Leader, Teacher-Designer, and a Teacher-Leader/Designer?

Activity 2: Updating your Personal Professional Mission Statement and Plan of Action.

Review the Personal Professional Mission Statement that you originally developed in chapter One. Considering the role of a Teacher-Leader/Designer, what modifications would you make to your Personal Professional Mission Statement? Are there any Teacher-Designer proposed goals that you can include in this statement? Provide a rationale for your additional information. Remember that a Personal Professional Mission Statement is an ever-evolving document that should be frequently referred to and revised when necessary. Thus, this current attempt should have "Draft" clearly stated at the top. Using this revised Personal Professional Mission Statement, review your Plan of Action and revise accordingly.

DISCUSSION QUESTIONS

1. How do teachers become leaders and designers? Are teachers naturally Teacher-Leader/Designers? Why or why not?

2. What if a fellow teacher asked you what a Teacher-Leader/Designer is? In one or two paragraphs, summarize what a Teacher-Leader/Designer does.

3. What are some of the characteristics of a Teacher-Leader/Designer that you already exhibit? What characteristics of a Teacher-Leader/Designer would you like to attain within the next year?

REFERENCES

Bishop, H. L., Tinley, A., & Berman, B. T. (1997). A contemporary leadership model to promote teacher leadership. *Action in Teacher Education, 19*(3), 77–81.

Bolman, L. G., & Deal, T. E. (1994). *Becoming a Teacher-Leader: From Isolation to Collaboration.* Thousand Oaks, CA: Corwin.

Ertmer, P. (1999). Addressing first- and second-order barriers to change: Strategies for technology integration. *Educational Technology Research and Development, 47*(4), 47–61.

Johnson, J., & Hynes, M. C. (1997). Teaching/learning/leading: Synonyms for change. *Action in Teacher Education, 19*(3), 107–119.

Katzenmeyer, M., & Moller, G. (2001). *Awakening the Sleeping Giant: Leadership Development for Teachers* (2nd ed.). Thousand Oaks, CA: Corwin.

Norman, D. (1988). *The psychology of everyday things.* New York: Basic Books.

O'Hair, M. J., & Reitzug, U. C. (1997). Teacher leadership: In what ways? For what purpose? *Action in Teacher Education, 19*(3), 65–76.

Petroski, H. (1985). *To Engineer is Human: The Role of Failure in Successful Design.* New York: St. Martin's.

Sugar, W., Crawley, F., & Fine, B. (2004). Examining teachers' decisions to adopt new technology. *Educational Technology and Society, 7*(4), 201–213.

Essential Skills of Teacher-Leader/ Designers

Chapter 4

Effective Communication Skills

This chapter will explore the importance of effective communication for Teacher-Leader/Designers. It will provide a definition and description of communication skills, and examine examples or models of the associated skills and processes. This chapter will provide readers with information that helps them understand the importance of effective communication.

After reading this chapter, you will be able to:

1. Define communication.
2. Describe why effective communication is important.
3. Measure effective communication.
4. Describe how to be a better communicator.
5. Define active listening.
6. Describe factors that interfere with effective communication.
7. List ways to improve communication skills.
8. Describe the importance of nonverbal communication.
9. Describe the role of facial expressions and body language in communication.
10. Describe the importance of written communication.

WHAT IS COMMUNICATION?

Communication is a broad concept that can be difficult to define. The word communication comes from the Latin word, *communico,* meaning "to share" or "to make common." In this context, communication is the giving and receiving of a language, which may be expressed through speech, writing, or symbolism. It is crucial for Teacher-Leader/Designers to have good communication skills to teach effectively, to connect with those who have a vested interest in students' educational outcomes (e.g., parents, administrators), and to bring people together. Also, communication is essential to sustain the school's culture and to build the strong, positive working relationships that are so essential for positive educational outcomes. In short, communication helps to determine the quality of human relationships and the ability to communicate effectively is an important characteristic of a successful Teacher-Leader/Designer.

WHY IS EFFECTIVE COMMUNICATION IMPORTANT?

A great deal of a teacher's professional life involves communication. On average, teachers are engaged in communication in one form or another for 70 percent of their day (Hinds & Pankake, 1987). There is a strong relationship between effective teacher communication and student achievement, as well as student satisfaction with instruction (Cruickshank, 1985; Hines, Cruickshank, & Kennedy, 1985). For leaders in general, the majority of their time also is spent on communication. It has been estimated that leaders in all capacities spend 66 percent to 78 percent of their time communicating (Hanna & Wilson, 1991). Needless to say, effective communication skills are fundamental to successful leaders including Teacher-Leader/Designers because such skills are needed throughout the day.

Not only are effective communication skills critical in educating students, but they are also necessary in working with colleagues to influence and direct them toward positive outcomes that you believe are necessary and important. Because communication accounts for a significant part of the day, it is critical that Teacher-Leader/Designers are clear with the messages they send as well as those they receive and interpret (Goldhaber, 1990). How often can conflicts, hurt feelings, or missed opportunities be attributed to poor communication? It likely occurs more often than you would like to admit! A great deal of time, energy, and resources may be lost due to ineffective communication.

"Seek first to understand, then to be understood," is an important component of effective communication, according to Stephen Covey (1994, p. 239). What does this statement mean to you? What are the typical outcomes when someone does not understand you? How do these outcomes make you feel? How do they impact your interpersonal relationships? It is important to respect all professional relationships, because "When people care about a relationship, they tend to communicate better than when they don't" (Geddes, 1995, p. 5). You may not like a certain colleague, administrator, parent, or other individual, but you should care about the professional relationship, because it allows for a more productive and fulfilling professional career. Communicating in a respectful manner with all people is a hallmark characteristic of Teacher-Leader/Designers.

Second to physical survival, Covey (1989) observes that, "the greatest need of a human being is psychological survival—to be understood, to be affirmed, to be validated, to be appreciated" (p. 241). When you communicate with someone and you actively listen to their input, you are providing validation for that person. Then you can focus on positive tasks such as influencing or problem-solving.

Communication is a complex, two-way process involving encoding, translation, and decoding of messages. Encoding are the ideas that the sender wishes to transmit and decoding is the translation of a received message into a perceived or interpreted meaning. Effective communication requires the communicator to translate his message in a way that is specifically tailored for his intended audience (i.e., students, colleagues, parents, administrators, legislators). For example, a Teacher-Leader/Designer would probably use different terminology when discussing a new teaching strategy with a parent as opposed to a colleague. Therefore, it is important that Teacher-Leader/Designers know their audiences when communicating so that their message can be put into the proper context.

THE STEPS OF EFFECTIVE COMMUNICATION

How does effective communication occur? One way is to understand the many steps that are involved in the communication process. It begins with the message that the presenter thinks has been conveyed, followed by what the presenter actually said. Next, the listener interprets what was said. Based on what the listener heard, a response is given, followed by what the listener actually said. The presenter's interpretation of the listener's words is followed by an action or outcome, which determines the success of the communication process. As one can see, the communication process is a complex, rapid, and fluid process (Conrad, 1985).

HOW TO BE A BETTER COMMUNICATOR

Most everyone would like to be a better communicator. As stated earlier, communication is quite a complex process. So how does one begin to improve communication skills? The first step is to attend to the nonverbal and verbal aspects of communication. According to Malandro and colleagues (1989), 80 percent of human communication is nonverbal. Nonverbal communication occurs in several ways. Three primary categories of nonverbal communications are (1) body movements, such as facial expressions, eye contact, posture, and gestures; (2) vocal cues such as tone of voice and the pacing or flow of speech; and (3) spatial relations, which include the physical distance between the participants (Friend & Cook, 2000). Thus, it goes without saying that nonverbal communication is a highly significant part of the communication process. Therefore, it is important that Teacher-Leader/Designers' nonverbal communication skills are congruent with their verbal communication skills, otherwise they may be sending mixed messages that can easily be misinterpreted.

For effective verbal communication, speak clearly and audibly, but not loudly. The tone of the voice should be warm and inviting. Samovar and Porter (1994) recommend modulating your voice to reflect nuances of feelings and the emotional tone of your message. To avoid miscommunication, use moderate speech tempo, and try to avoid the following pitfalls when speaking: mumbling or speaking inaudibly; monotone voice; halting speech; frequent grammatical errors; prolonged silences; excessively animated speech; slow, rapid, or staccato speech; nervous laughter; constant throat clearing; speaking loudly; and use of lingo or faddish sayings.

One type of effective communication strategy encompasses paraphrasing, clarifying, and reflecting as opposed to parroting. For example, when using this strategy, an effective communicator would say: "The problem as you see it . . .", or "This is your decision and the reasons are . . .", or "If I understand you correctly, you are saying that we should . . .", or "You feel strongly that . . .", or "Let me repeat what I think you said. . . ."

Reformulating is another effective communication strategy. For example, an effective communicator would say, "We seem to agree on certain points, but we need further clarification on the following points. . . ." Questioning is important and questions should be formulated to be supportive, positively phrased, and open-ended. When providing feedback, Teacher-Leader/Designers should be nonjudgmental, nonevaluative, specific, and immediate (Person & Spitzberg, 1987). For a positive outcome to occur, the skill of active listening must be part of the communication process.

Listening Skills

Teacher-Leader/Designers will find that active listening is an essential communication skill. Many people think they are good listeners and feel that they do not require formal instruction on how to listen. However, good listening skills must be learned and most people have not had any type of training in listening (Covey, 1994). According to Towne (2004), listening is a skill that many of us can improve upon. The skill of active listening occurs when the listener is actively engaged in hearing what the speaker is saying.

Active listening requires concentration and focus. The listener should stop what he is doing and give the speaker his full attention. Distractions should be minimized, but if this is not possible, then schedule a time when the conversation will not be interrupted. Active listening is essential because it conveys your interest in what the speaker has to say. It also encourages individuals to expand on their thinking. A good listener uses paraphrasing frequently. Paraphrasing checks and clarifies what the other person intended, before responding. Simple paraphrasing is repeating back exactly what is being said. This type of paraphrasing is useful in making sure you understand directions, expectations, and requests. Regular paraphrasing is stating your way what his/her remark conveys to you in order to test your understanding. Paraphrasing plus is when you paraphrase and then add your own thoughts or hunch onto the paraphase. This is used to pursue the fullest meaning and feelings of the other.

As a Teacher-Leader/Designer, people will come to you with problems that need to be addressed or solved. An effective Teacher-Leader/Designer will let others do the majority of the talking, while actively listening to what is being said. Often, when Teacher-Leader/Designers listen carefully to the problems of others and ask clarifying questions they can help others to clarify their problems on their own. This is important because clarifying a problem is a crucial step toward solving the problem (Lustig & Koester, 1993). Consequently, individuals seeking assistance may, be able to reach their own solutions, just by having the Teacher-Leader/ Designer actively listen to their problems. Those seeking help may even thank the Teacher-Leader/Designer for helping them solve their problems, when in reality the Teacher-Leader/Designer simply listened and provided an effective sounding board.

FACTORS THAT INTERFERE WITH EFFECTIVE LISTENING

During a discussion, people often stop listening to what is being said because they are too busy rehearsing a response for when it is their turn to speak. This potentially creates a problem in communication because the speaker's entire message has not been heard (Wolvin & Coakley, 1982). When this occurs, important details may be missed, resulting in miscommunication. Miscommunication can also occur when the listener is distracted or lost in thought, rather than being focused on what is being said.

Sometimes as listeners we filter messages being sent because we want to hear them in a certain context. We hear the message in our own context, rather than the context meant by the person sending the message. To allow effective communication, listeners must try to understand the viewpoint and perspective of the person sending the message (Hayakawa, 1978).

It is important not to become distracted by extraneous details during active listening. Active listening requires the listener to ascertain the relevant pieces of information and not waste time addressing non-relevant matters.

WAYS TO IMPROVE LISTENING SKILLS

Specific strategies can be employed to improve listening skills. One such strategy is to rehearse the information being conveyed to you by mentally paraphrasing and summarizing. Another strategy involves categorizing the information being received, and grouping together certain ideas and information as the message is delivered. This helps you sort and group the information in preparation for response. Some people find it helpful to note details in writing to use in developing a thoughtful, organized response. You may find it helpful to select and use a signal to hold your responses; this allows you to mentally store information prior to your response.

NONVERBAL COMMUNICATION

Nonverbal communication is expressed through facial expression, body posture, and other types of body language. When you are engaged in active listening, it is important to maintain desirable facial expressions (Malandro, Barker, & Barker, 1989). First and foremost, it is important to have direct eye contact (except when culturally proscribed) in order to connect with the person sending the message. Try to keep your eyes level with the speaker's. A facial expression that reflects warmth and concern helps significantly with active listening. Keep your facial muscles and mouth relaxed, and have varied and animated facial expressions, with an occasional genuine smile. This communicates to the speaker you are listening and responding to their words and that their message has made an impact.

UNDESIRABLE FACIAL EXPRESSIONS

Undesirable facial expressions, such as avoiding eye contact when listening to a speaker, can underline effective communication. For most people, avoiding eye contact communicates that the listener is not actively listening, especially if the individual is staring fixedly at something or someone other than the person talking. Other subtle expressions, such as lifting the eyebrows critically while listening communicates that the speaker's message is not being well received by the listener.

Active listeners should also try to avoid nodding the head excessively, which may communicate to the speaker that they are agreeing with what is being said even before it is expressed. Yawning, looking at a watch, and other expressions of disinterest communicate boredom or lack of concentration on what is being said (Hall, 1966). An unresponsive facial expression suggests that you are not comfortable, which decreases the likelihood of your being totally focused on what is being said. Active listeners should avoid an inappropriate slight smile or pursing or biting the lips because it sends the signal that you are disagreeing with what is being said.

THE IMPACT OF BODY LANGUAGE IN EFFECTIVE COMMUNICATION

Body language is a very powerful tool in effective communication (Mehrabian, 1981). Certain postures can convey the listener's openness and willingness to listen. Effective communicators should keep their arms and hands moderately expressive when speaking, and make appropriate gestures when listening. A rigid body position with arms tightly folded across the chest should always be avoided. The body should lean slightly forward toward the speaker, and should be in an attentive but relaxed posture. Never fidget, squirm, or slouch in a chair while another person is speaking. Do not cover the mouth with your hands or fingers. Finally, according to Lustig & Koester (1993), the desirable physical proximity between listener and speaker should be three to five feet. Excessive closeness or distance, or trying to talk across a desk or other barrier can hinder effective communication.

Knowledge of the effects and impact of nonverbal communication is needed, because our awareness may enhance favorable communication. Nonverbal cues may be unconsciously acted and reacted upon, regulating proximity, gestures, eye gaze and touch. Each component of nonverbal communication affects our relationship and interpersonal environment in intricate ways. Nonverbal cues provide insight into affect states, influence another's perception of an individual competence, persuasiveness, power, sincerity, and vulnerability.

WRITTEN COMMUNICATION

For Teacher-Leader/Designers, the written word remains an important means of communication. The challenge is to present an idea clearly and succinctly. There are many types of writing styles, but for the most part, Teacher-Leader/Designers engage in informative and persuasive writing.

Informative writing seeks to provide information and explain ideas. To be effective, informative writing should focus mainly on the subject being discussed, accompanied by an adequate amount of facts and details. Persuasive writing, on the other hand, seeks to convince the reader to embrace the writer's judgment or opinion. Persuasive writing focuses mainly on the reader, whom the writer wishes to influence. Effective persuasive writing does not merely state the writer's opinion. The reader expects the author to offer convincing support for her point of view. Thus, the writer's point of view must be supported with adequate information that explains and defends the idea being discussed.

To be effective, informative, and persuasive with your writing, you need to consider your readers. Good writing is often judged by its ability to reach its intended audience. First and foremost, consider your audience's background. What can you assume the audience already knows? For example, a written report filled with education jargon assumes that the audience is familiar with this specialized vocabulary. However, an audience of state legislators might have trouble understanding such a report. Rewriting your report in lay terms would make it more accessible to legislators and other non-educators.

It is important to be organized when communicating writing. Be as brief and clear as possible. Know what you want to convey to whom, and why you want to convey it as succinctly as possible. Always keep the reader in mind, and remember that readers differ in their language skills, needs, and expectations, as well as their openness and readiness for communication. Finally, write in a professional manner, because what you write is a reflection of you.

SUMMARY

Effective communication skills are key to being a successful Teacher-Leader/Designer. Communication occurs when individuals interact with each other. Communication is a complex and fluid process, so it is important to be aware of how each aspect of the process contributes to the process, including the influence of nonverbal communication as well as active listening. Most everyone's communication skills could be improved. When people work toward improving their communication skills they will likely experience less frustration and more success in their interactions with others. The outcomes of effective communication will be productive, positive, and wonderful.

CASE STUDY

Alice Jaramillo is a student teacher in an inner-city school in which the majority of students receive free or reduced-price lunch. Alice is the first student teacher that Mrs. Wellesley has had in her eighth grade math class. Currently, Alice is having some problems with classroom management that she needs to discuss with Mrs. Wellesley. Whenever the two women hold a conference, Alice leaves frustrated because she doesn't think Mrs. Wellesley listens to her. Alice feels that all Mrs. Wellesley does is lecture to her without providing any suggestions in how to deal effectively with the situation. Every time Alice starts to speak, Mrs. Wellesley interrupts her. At other times when Alice tries to talk with Mrs. Wellesley, she does not give Alice her full attention. Consequently, Alice has given up in seeking help from her supervising teacher. What suggestions would you give to Alice and Mrs. Wellesley to try to improve this situation?

ACTIVITIES

1. Identify two or three settings where your communication skills are necessary to your success as a Teacher-Leader/Designer. This list may include conducting meetings, holding a parent-teacher conference, presenting to the local school, etc.

2. Over the next two weeks, keep a journal on your own communication skills. Identify two instances where you communicated well and two that did not go as well as you would have liked.

3. Practice your active listening skills. Videotape yourself in various circumstances that involve your communication skills. Analyze your listening skills, paying special attention to your facial expressions and body language.

DISCUSSION QUESTIONS

1. Why do you think most people are poor communicators and poor listeners?

2. What are the implications when someone tells you, "I know what you are thinking, but you're wrong!" How does such a statement make you feel?

3. Identify the different people and groups that a Teacher-Leader/Designer communicates with during the school year? Which people and groups are easier to communicate with and which can be more challenging? Why?

REFERENCES

Conrad, C. (1985). *Strategic Organizational Communication: Cultures, Situations, and Adaptations.* New York: Holt, Rinehart, & Winston.

Covey, S. R. (1989). *The 7 Habits of Highly Effective People.* New York: Simon & Schuster.

Cruickshank, D. (1985). Applying research on teacher clarity. *Journal of Teacher Education, 35*(2), 44–48.

Friend, M., & Cook, L. (2000). *Interactions: Collaboration Skills for School Professionals* (3rd ed.). New York: Longman.

Geddes, D. S. (1995). *Keys to Communication: A Handbook for School Success.* Thousand Oaks, CA: Corwin.

Goldhaber, F. (1990). *Organizational Communication* (5th ed.). Dubuque, IA: Brown.

Hall, E. (1966). *The Hidden Dimension.* Garden City, NY: Doubleday.

Hanna, M., & Wilson, G. (1991). *Communicating in Business and Professional Settings* (3rd ed.). New York: McGraw-Hill.

Hayakawa, S. (1978). *Language in Thought and Action* (4th ed.). New York: Harcourt, Brace, Jovanovich.

Hinds, A., & Pankake, A. (1987). Listening: The missing side of school communication. *Clearing House, 60*(6), 281–283.

Hines, A., Cruickshank, D., & Kennedy, J. (1985). Teacher clarity and its relationship to student achievement and satisfaction. *American Education Research Journal, 22,* 87–99.

Lustig, M., & Koester, J. (1993). *Intercultural Competence: Interpersonal Communication Across Cultures.* New York: Harper's College Division.

Malandro, L., Barker, L., & Barker, D. (1989). *Nonverbal Communication* (2nd ed.). New York: Random House.

Mehrabian, A. (1981). Silent *Messages: Implicit Communication of Emotions and Attitudes* (2nd ed.). New York: Random House.

Person, J., & Spitzberg, B. (1987). *Interpersonal Communication: Concepts, Components, and Contexts* (2nd ed.). Dubuque, IA: Brown.

Samovar, A., & Porter, R. (1994). *Intercultural Communication: A reader* (7th ed.). Belmont, CA: Wadsworth.

Towne, N. (2004). *Looking Out/Looking In* (11th ed.). Belmont, CA: Wadsworth.

Wolvin, A., & Coakley, C. (1982). *Listening* (3rd ed.). Dubuque, IA: Brown.

Chapter 5

Effective Presentation Skills

This chapter discusses the reasons why effective presentations skills are necessary and what steps are needed to develop and deliver powerful presentations. The ability to communicate and share your ideas to a wide range of audiences is essential for being a successful Teacher-Leader/Designer. Effective presentations do not just happen, but rather are the result of fulfilling important criteria in order to accomplish goals. This chapter describes the steps and basic components of a well-developed presentation as well as why possessing this skill is important for Teacher-Leader/Designers.

After reading this chapter, you will be able to:

1. Describe why possessing presentation skills are important.
2. Plan an effective presentation.
3. Prepare an effective presentation.
4. Describe how to open a presentation.
5. Describe how to maintain interest during the presentation.
6. Describe how to respond to questions from the audience.
7. Describe how to close the presentation.
8. List important points to remember during a presentation.
9. Describe how to effectively use visuals.

WHY IS POSSESSING PRESENTATION SKILLS IMPORTANT?

Teacher-Leader/Designers often must stand before colleagues, parents, administrators, community leaders, legislators, and others to present ideas and information. The primary focus of a presentation is to enlighten, teach, discuss, or persuade (Allotey, 2003; Farr, 2000). Although the content of a presentation is important, the ability to prepare and deliver information effectively is crucial. Possessing exemplary presentation skills is a necessary characteristic of a dynamic Teacher-Leader/Designer (Brookfield, 1990). There are several essential components that must be addressed in all effective presentations.

PLANNING THE PRESENTATION

Proper planning is the first step in beginning an effective presentation. Foremost, you must have a thorough grasp of the content. When you have a strong working knowledge of the content, you can present with confidence and discuss the topic in depth and at length, as well as address possible questions, confusion, misconceptions, or skepticism from the audience (Schmalz & Moliterno, 2001; Wu, 1987). Furthermore, you must believe in and support the merit of the content if you are to be an advocate for a new idea or program.

As you plan for the presentation, it is important to consider who will be attending the presentation as well as the reason for their attendance (Mills, 1991; Sarnoff, 1981). People attend presentations for various reasons, such as interest, curiosity, a genuine desire to learn, or possibly because it is mandatory. Once you are aware of your audience, you will have a better chance of being properly prepared. Other issues that an effective presenter should consider are a sensitivity to the vocabulary and terminology that will be used and the degree of the audience's prior knowledge of, or experience with, the topic. In addition, you should predetermine the tone of the presentation. Will it be formal or informal?

The amount of time that is allotted for your presentation will significantly impact on your presentation, because it will determine its depth and pace (Gramston, 1991; Smith, 1995). When time is limited, you will be able to touch on only the highlights and essentials of the topic, whereas more time allows you to deliver more content, provide group work, and allow for breaks.

Whatever the amount of time you are given, the pace of the presentation is important. Do not rush or overwhelm the audience with too much information to process (Maynard, 1997). It is better to provide the audience with only the critical pieces of information necessary for comprehension.

Focus is key to an effective presentation. The best way to maintain focus is to clearly define your objectives. The objectives should drive the presentation (Nicholls, 1999). Every piece of information delivered, every example provided, every activity the members of the audience participate in should be ordered to meet the objectives. Ideally the objectives of the presentation should be articulated at the beginning and revisited at its conclusion. This process helps to reinforce your message for the audience.

PREPARING THE PRESENTATION

Typically, presentations are given to inform, teach, or persuade. It is important to clarify why you are giving the presentation in order to help you focus on how to properly prepare for it (Corbett, 1992; Sharp, 1993). If the purpose of the presentation is to inform, then you will probably provide graphs, charts, and other data to help the audience understand the content. If the purpose is to teach a new skill or concept, then you might include small group activities that will allow the participants opportunities to learn by practicing aspects of the skill or concept being taught. However, if your purpose is to persuade a group of people, you may want to prepare a PowerPoint presentation that provides evidence or supports future projections. Whatever the purpose of your presentation, proper preparation is key.

Organization is essential to delivering an effective presentation! As discussed earlier, a presentation should be focused and centered on clearly defined objectives (Gramston, 1992). In addition, information should be efficiently presented so as not to waste time. If your audience senses that you are disorganized and perceives that their time is being wasted due to your lack of organizational skills, then your presentation will probably be unsuccessful. An outline is a useful organizational tool in preparing for a presentation and is highly recommended.

Make sure all collateral material, such as handouts, charts, overheads, PowerPoints, and videos used during the presentation are neat, well-crafted, and carefully proofread. These materials will enhance your presentation, but it is absolutely imperative that they are free of mistakes and have a professional and polished look (Raines, 1989). Errors in presentation materials reflect poorly upon you and undermine your credibility. Appearance does make a difference in the effectiveness of a presentation (Meilach, 1992; Satterthwaite, 1990).

IMPORTANT POINTS TO REMEMBER ABOUT PRESENTING

The delivery of the presentation is determined by you, the presenter (Abernathy, 1999). Try to capture your audience's attention with a strong opening, for example, by providing an unbelievable fact or a joke (Feigelson, 1987). Pace your talk appropriately to positively impact the response from your audience. Include pauses and gestures to emphasize the important points of the presentation (Sharp, 1993). Keep transitions smooth and logical, and maintain an even flow. If the presentation is lengthy, periodically review the main points to help keep the audience on track. The conclusion of the presentation should summarize the main points. Finally, never exceed the allotted time! It is imperative that you remain cognizant of time throughout the presentation, because your audience certainly will.

Practice, practice, practice! It is important that you rehearse your presentation at least once before you actually deliver it (Mandel, 1987). If possible, this rehearsal should occur at the location of the actual presentation. If that is not possible, then visualize the room and imagine the audience in it. Give the presentation to a trusted colleague or other individual who will give you constructive feedback. One helpful hint: Occasionally start somewhere in the middle of your presentation while you practice.

THE DAY OF THE PRESENTATION

On the day of the presentation, check out the room in which you will be presenting. Prepare the room at least fifteen minutes before you expect participants to arrive. Make sure all the equipment you need is in place and in working order. Nothing can disrupt a presentation like a burnt out overhead projector bulb! Greet the participants as they arrive. Shake hands with them and introduce yourself. This helps you to establish a connection with your audience before you begin the actual presentation (Lambert, 1988). For large audiences, a microphone will help to ensure that everyone will hear you, as well as save your voice. (Make sure that you have some water to sip on during the presentation.) During the presentation, avoid standing behind the podium; try to get as close as you can to the audience. Finally, find a mirror and double check your appearance before the presentation!

THE ACTUAL PRESENTATION

When the time finally arrives for your presentation to begin and you are being introduced, be sure and take several deep breaths and smile. A smile creates a positive impression of you and your presentation even before you speak one word. Try to keep smiling throughout your presentation. Give your opening statement and follow it by clearly describing the objectives of the presentation (Carter & Powell, 1992). During the presentation, use a natural and moderate rate of speech. Avoid pause fillers such as "um," "uh," or "Okay," and distracting behavior, such as pacing back and forth or fumbling with change in your pocket.

Be enthusiastic and positive from the beginning to the end of the presentation. Make eye contact with individuals in the audience, but do not stare at one section or person in particular. Avoid any criticism or negative comments, and keep your presentation upbeat! Do not allow interruptions to throw you off course. If an individual interrupts repeatedly during the presentation, simply respond politely in a professional manner that you will be happy to discuss their concerns and questions in greater detail at break or at the end of the presentation.

Presenting information in a variety of ways will help keep your presentation fresh and help increase audience attention, retention, and participation (Moye & Rodgers, 1987). The more opportunities you provide for your audience to be actively involved in the presentation the better! Your visuals should be in at least two different formats, so if you experience technology problems and cannot use your PowerPoint, you should have overheads available as a back-up.

As stated earlier, be cognizant of the time allotted to you. Let the audience know what to expect at the beginning of the presentation and what time it will end. It is important that you restate the objectives of the presentation at the conclusion. Just as you need a strong opening statement, your presentation will need a strong conclusion. The beginning, and especially the ending, of your presentation will be what the audience remembers! Finally, it is important to remember that being flexible and keeping your cool is a must when presenting. Be prepared for the unexpected and respond in a poised and professional manner.

ANSWERING QUESTIONS

Addressing audience questions will always be part of a presentation. Decide ahead of time when you will take questions during the presentation. Let the audience know whether you will address questions during and at the end of the presentation, or only at the end of the presentation. It is usually best to address only those questions during the presentation that will clear up any misunderstanding or ambiguity. However, regardless of when a question is asked, it is important that you repeat it so that everyone can hear it (Saxl, Lieberman, & Miles, 1987). When answering a question, make sure that you understand it and take a moment to think through how you will respond. Keep your responses succinct and to the point. Avoid prolonged discussions with just one person, and under no circumstances should you engage in an argument. Remember to keep it positive! Finally, if you are unable to answer any question, be honest and simply state that you are unable to address the question at the present time.

AFTER THE PRESENTATION

At the conclusion of your presentation, there are several things to do before you leave the room. First, take a deep breath, congratulate yourself, and collect your thoughts. Often, there will be members from the audience who will approach you and want to speak with you individually. Once again, try to keep these conversations brief, and make a later appointment for conversations requiring more time. Be sure to collect your belongings, keeping everything as organized as possible, and make sure all equipment is turned off. That's it for the presentation. If you promised to do some follow-up work or to send related materials to members of the audience, do so in a timely manner.

SUMMARY

Teacher-Leader/Designers often will have many ideas they wish to share with groups of people through presentations. Presenting to an audience in an effective and polished manner will have a greater impact on the participants. A presentation requires proper planning and preparation. It is important to organize the presentation with a logical flow of the major points. Consider your audience and their knowledge and experience with the topic being presented, and tailor the presentation accordingly. During the presentation, be enthusiastic, positive, and energetic. Make sure the pacing is appropriate, and always begin and end on time.

CASE STUDY

Delores Cruz is scheduled to do a presentation on a reading strategy that she has developed and implemented in her classroom at a state level professional conference for reading teachers. The reading strategy she has developed has been phenomenally successful in her classroom and she has shared it with colleagues in her school who, in turn, have experienced the same high rate of success. Delores is very excited with this opportunity to share this strategy before a statewide audience of reading teachers and hopes they will want to implement it in their schools. The presentation is scheduled for 10:00 a.m. Delores has trouble locating the room she has been assigned to present in and arrives just minutes before her scheduled start time. She rushes into the room and immediately begins her presentation without catching her breath. She has so much she wants to share that she isn't sure where to begin. Members of the audience begin to ask questions, and Delores becomes flustered and loses her train of thought. As luck would have it, the overhead projector does not work. As she is dealing with the equipment, she notices people from the audience slipping through the doorway and leaving the presentation. Delores feels defeated! What could she have done to prevent the failure of her presentation?

ACTIVITIES

1. Attend a presentation and critique it. What were its strengths? What are some factors that could have enhanced the presentation?

2. Generate a list of activities and strategies to actively involve the audience during a presentation.

DISCUSSION QUESTIONS

1. Identify two or three of the most recent presentations that you have attended. What are the five things you remember most about each presentation? Why do you think you remember those particular components?

2. Which is more important: your perceptions of the audience or the audience's perception of you? Why?

REFERENCES

Abernathy, D. J. (1999). Presentation tips from the pros. *Training & Development, 53*(10), 19–20.

Allotey, J. (2003). Presentation skills. *Nurse Researcher, 11*(1), 86–92.

Brookfield, S. (1990). *The Skillful Teacher.* San Francisco: Jossey-Bass.

Carter, M., & Powell, D. (1992). Teacher leaders as staff developers. *Journal of Staff Development, 13,* 8–12.

Corbett, A. H. (1992). Give participants responsibility for learning: Techniques for opening a workshop. *Journal of Staff Development, 13,* 40–42.

Farr, J. V. (2000). Developing your oral communication skills. *Journal of Management in Engineering, 16*(6), 6–10.

Feigelson, S. B. (1987). Boring meetings? Put humor to work! *Journal of Staff Development, 8,* 63–66.

Gramston, R. (1991). Notes on the persuasive art of presenting: Openers. *Developer, 3,* 7–9.

Gramston, R., & Wellman, B. (1992). *How to Make Presentations that Teach and Transform.* Alexandria, VA: Association for Supervision and Curriculum Development.

Lambert, L. (1988). Staff development redesigned. *Phi Delta Kappa, 69,* 665–668.

Mandel, S. (1987). *Effective Presentation Skills.* Los Altos, CA: Crisp.

Maynard, R. (1997). Turn up the volume, tune in to the audience. *Nation's Business, 85*(6), 10–14.

Meilach, D. Z. (1992). Overhead transparencies designed to communicate. *Arts & Activities,* 42–50.

Mills, S. (1990). Planning a workshop? *Developer, 1,* 7.

Moye, M. J., & Rodgers, K. M. (1987). Teachers as staff developers: A success story. *Journal of Staff Development, 8,* 42–44.

Nicholls, P. (1999). Logic and marbles: Presentation skills yesterday and today. *Computers in Libraries, 19*(4), 57–61.

Raines, C. (1989). *Visual Aids in Business.* Los Altos, CA: Crisp.

Satterthwaite, L. (1990). *Instructional Media: Materials Production and Utilization* (3rd ed.). Dubuque, IA: Kendall/Hunt.

Sarnoff, D. (1981). *Make the Most of your Best.* New York: Doubleday.

Saxl, E., Lieberman, A., & Miles, M. (1987). Help is at hand: New knowledge for teachers as staff developers. *Journal of Staff Development, 8,* 7–11.

Schmalz, K., & Moliterno, A. (2001). *Developing Presentation Skills: A Guide for Effective Instruction.* Boston: Allyn & Bacon.

Sharp, P. A. (1993). *Sharing your good ideas.* Portsmouth, NH: Heinemann.

Smith, D. (1995). Powerful presentation skills. *Women in Business, 47*(2), 32–36.

Wu, P. C. (1987). Teachers as staff developers: Research, opinions and cautions. *Journal of Staff Development, 8,* 4–6.

Chapter 6

Effective Technology Skills

This chapter will explore the importance of acquiring and developing effective technology for Teacher-Leader/Designers. It will provide a definition and description of instructional media, instructional technology, and the interrelationship between these two concepts, as well as the relationship between instructional media and instructional methods. This chapter will discuss a hierarchy of essential instructional media characteristics and known incentives and obstacles that affect instructional technology use. This chapter will examine the factors involved with adopting innovations and how to measure effective technology use, and will discuss the role of a technology facilitator within the schools. It also will provide readers with information that helps them understand the importance of effective technology skills.

After reading this chapter, you will be able to:

1. Define instructional technology and instructional media.
2. Describe the relationship between instructional technology and instructional media.
3. Describe the relationship between instructional media and instructional methods.
4. Define Dale's Cone of Experience.
5. Describe factors that interfere with effective instructional technology.
6. Describe the five phases of adopting innovations.
7. Define the adopter roles within respect to adopting innovations.
8. Describe why effective technology skills are important.
9. Describe how to measure effective technology use.
10. Describe how to become a better technology user.
11. Define the role of a technology facilitator within a school setting.

WHAT IS TECHNOLOGY?

This section will discuss the nature of technology within instructional settings. However, we must first distinguish between instructional media and instructional technology. Understanding this difference will inform our perspective of technology and how it influences the role of a Teacher-Leader/Designer.

What exactly is instructional media and how does it relate to technology within instructional settings? To establish a working definition, we list the instructional media used in our respective classes during the past few years, including the following: computers, DVDs, overhead transparencies, PowerPoint slideshows, and other related items. You probably anticipated this list of possible instructional media and probably have either used this instructional media in your own classrooms, or perhaps have seen some of this instructional media in a previous class. However, a list of possible instructional media also could have included paintbrushes, a soccer ball, a hammer, darts, and other related items.

We suspect that you will find this new list more perplexing, so we will explain. Heinich and colleagues (2001) define medium as "a means of communication. Derived from the Latin *medium* ("between"), the term refers to anything that carries information between a source and a receiver." Thus, an instructional medium (plural, media) is a means of communication to carry information between a source (e.g., teacher) and a receiver (e.g., student) for instructional purposes. We can conceivably use our seemingly perplexing list of instructional media to communicate instruction between a teacher and a student. For example, if a physical education teacher wanted to teach intermediate soccer skills to a group of seventh-grade students, she would use a soccer ball to communicate this information. If a high school construction technology instructor wanted to teach ninth- and tenth-grade students how to build a birdhouse, he would use a hammer as a means to communicate this information. Essentially, any object that is used to communicate information from an instructor to a learner for instructional purposes is considered instructional media.

What is technology and how does it relate to instructional media? Instructional media can be any object used to communicate within an instructional setting, whereas instructional technology is a *set of knowledge* applied to solve a particular solution. Yes, that is correct: Technology is not an object (e.g., computer), but a set of knowledge. John Galbraith noted that technology is "the systematic application of scientific and organized knowledge to practical tasks" (Heinich, et al., 2001). The Oxford English Dictionary defines technology as "the branch of knowledge that deals with the mechanical arts or applied sciences" (Oxford University Press, 2002). Too often, there is a misperception that technology is an object (e.g., DVD) and instructional technology is equated with instructional media. However, instructional technology actually is an application of a set of knowledge to practical tasks within instructional settings.

Some educators may have difficulty in viewing instructional technology as an application of a set of knowledge to practical tasks within instructional settings. For clarification purposes in understanding the role of the

Teacher-Leader/Designer, we would like to adopt a definition that combines the definitions of both instructional media and instructional technology. With this bundled definition, we intend to address how enhanced technology skills can prepare Teacher-Leader/Designers for success. Our technology definition is comparable to Reigeluth's (1996) distinction between hard technologies and soft technologies. Hard technologies are actual objects (e.g., computers) or essentially instructional media. Soft technologies represent a set of knowledge that provides solutions to practical tasks. For instance, Reigeluth advocates school restructuring based upon systemic change principles. His plan would be considered a soft technology.

THE RELATIONSHIP BETWEEN INSTRUCTIONAL MEDIA AND INSTRUCTIONAL METHODS

Another perspective of the role of instructional technology and instructional media is found in Figure 6.1. This graphic depicts the relationship of the communication between the instructor and student(s) involving me-

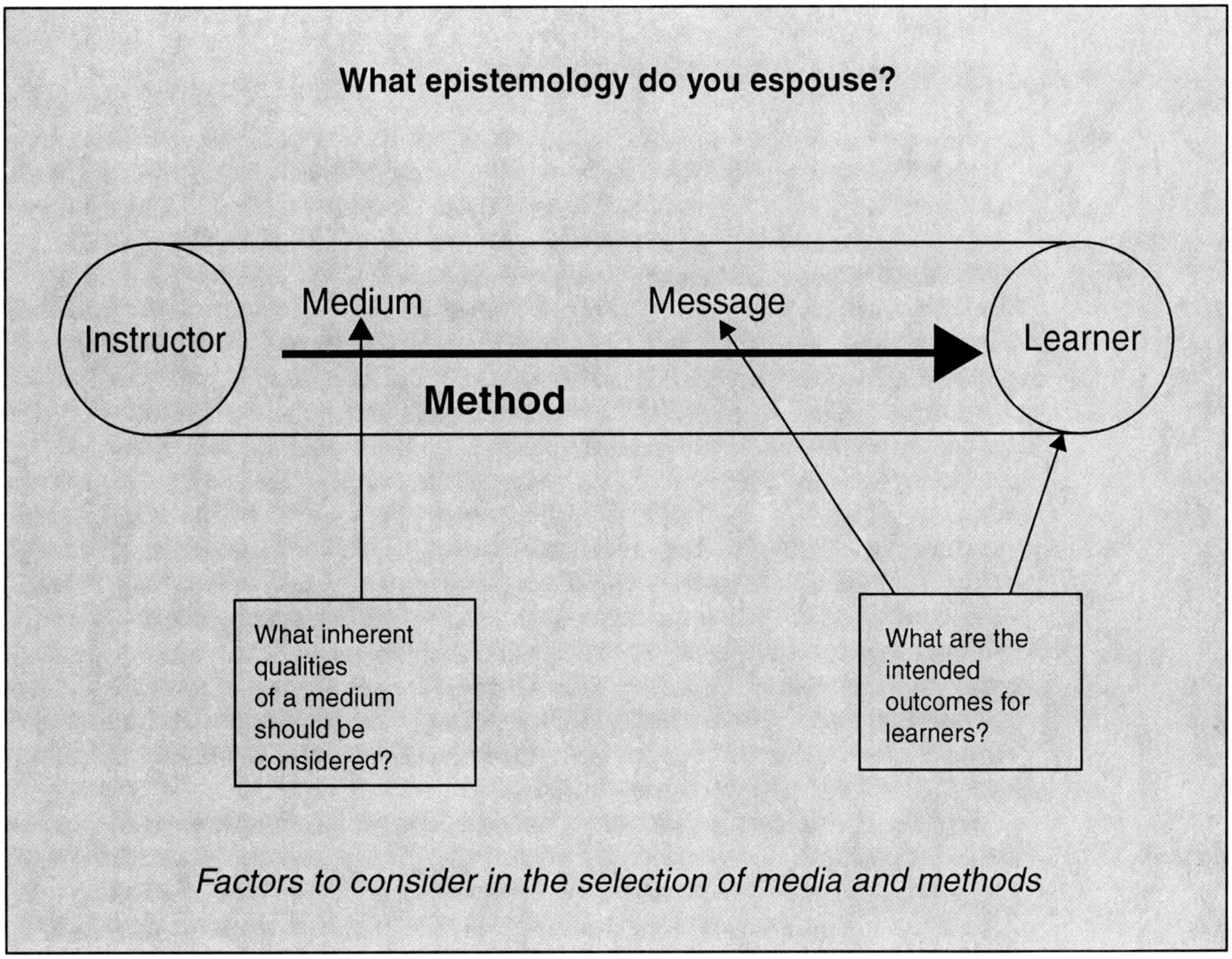

Figure 6.1 Relationship between instructional media and instructional methods.

dia, methods, and the message. Essentially, it illustrates the critical factors involved with selecting the appropriate instructional media and methods. One must ask, "What inherent qualities of a medium should be considered?" That is, are there any specific characteristics of a particular instructional media that will influence how instruction would take place? Also, with regards to the particular message (e.g., fourth-grade students learning fractions), one must ask, "What are the intended outcomes of the learner?" The answer will definitively influence the selection of the particular media and methods that are used to teach the particular message. Influencing the entire decision of selection of media and methods is related to one's own epistemology or educational philosophy. Several epistemologies (e.g., behaviorism, constructivism) are available to choose from and they play an important role in this decision.

This discourse about the relationship between instructional media and methods demonstrates the need to focus on developing effective instructional methods as opposed to exclusively focusing on the actual instructional media (Ely, 1963). The overall intent of instructional technology is to develop the most appropriate solution to the given practical problem by proposing effective methods and media that enable effective learning experiences to achieve learner competence and understanding.

EDGAR DALE'S CONE OF EXPERIENCE

Another perspective of technology that is advantageous for Teacher-Leader/Designers is Edgar Dale's Cone of Experience (see Figure 6.2). In his seminal book, *Audiovisual Methods in Teaching* (1969), Dale devised this graphic as a way to describe the relationship between specific instructional media and types of knowledge. You will note that the apex of the cone contains "verbal symbols," "visual symbols," etc. At the bottom of the cone, you will find "direct, purposeful experiences," "contrived experiences," etc. Dale postulated that the media used at the top of the cone were best suited for teaching abstract knowledge (e.g., the Theory of Relativity), whereas the media at the bottom of the cone were best suited for teaching concrete knowledge (e.g., how to create a basic Web page). Thus, verbal symbols (i.e., someone who is talking to students) and visual symbols (e.g., printed words in an e-mail message) are best suited to teach abstract knowledge. Conversely, direct, purposeful experiences (i.e., internships) and contrived experiences (e.g., a simulation) are best used to teach concrete knowledge. Teacher-Leader/Designers can use Dale's Cone as a guide to determine which media to use. If one wants to teach abstract knowledge, one would choose from among the media at the top of the cone. If one wants to teach concrete knowledge, one would choose from among media at the bottom of the cone.

Dale's overall purpose was to facilitate what he characterized as *Permanent Learning*. He observed, "As today's teachers face this problem of forgetting, they wonder whether up-to-date instructional methods and materials . . . can transform classroom instruction in a series of rich, *memorable* experiences" (1969, p. 38). Dale's Cone of various instructional media provides the opportunity for Teacher-Leader/Designers to make a

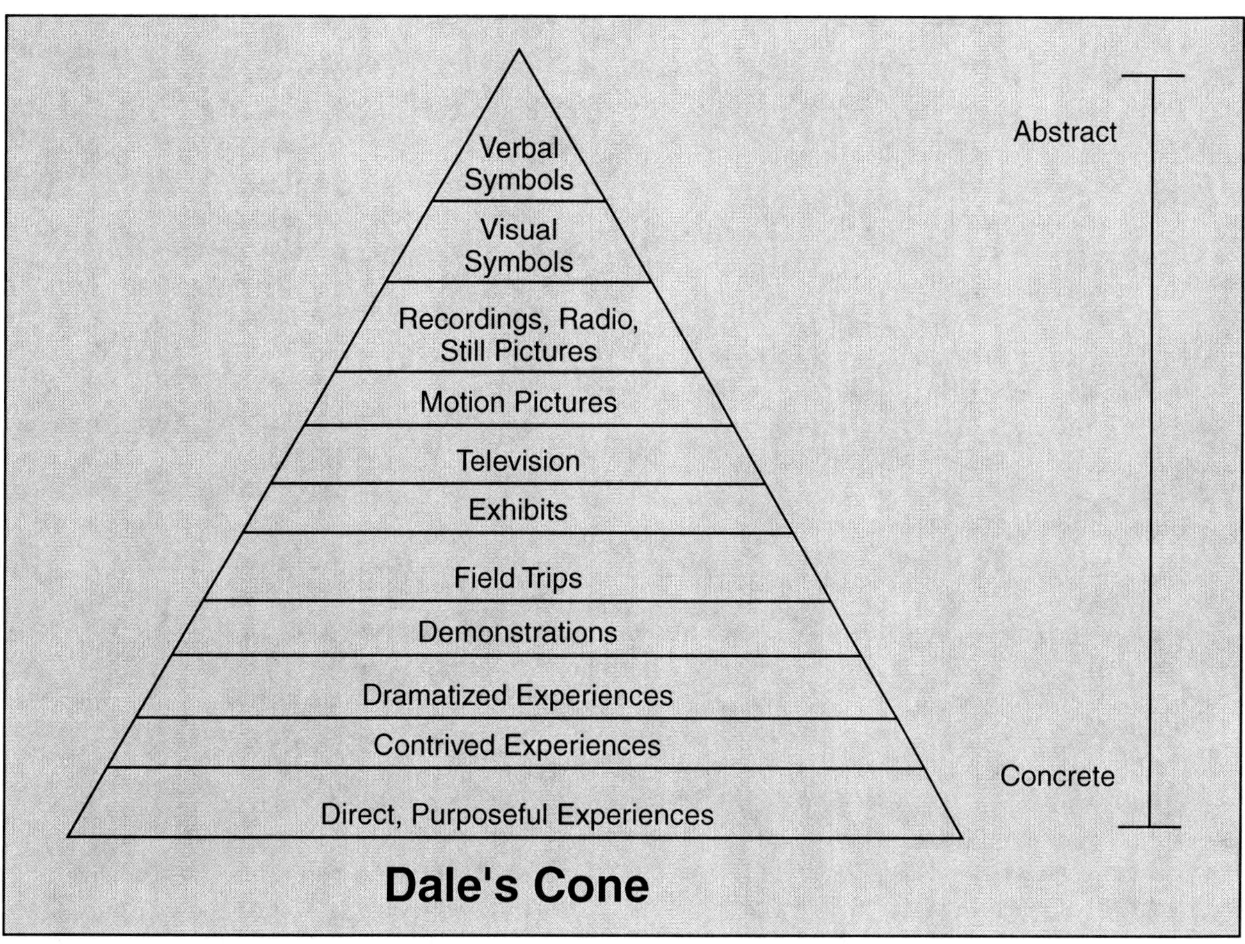

Figure 6.2 Dale's Cone of Experiences.

conscious decision about selecting effective instructional media. The focus is not on deciding the most current and fashionable media, but on ensuring students will be able have rich, usable learning experiences and have meaningful associations with the content. According to Dale, this process leads to permanent learning.

FACTORS THAT INTERFERE WITH EFFECTIVE TECHNOLOGY USE

Several factors can interfere with Teacher-Leader/Designers' effective technology use. Table 6.1 shows a detailed list of incentives and obstacles that can be used to adopt and integrate technology within schools. Some obvious, tangible factors include additional resources, financial support, and staff development. Teachers also need to be convinced that a particular technology will solve their problems through practical means (Cuban, 1986, p. 66). Some of these proposed improvements include promoting teacher empowerment (Topp, Mortenson, & Grandgenett, 1995, p. 11), providing a comfortable atmosphere and individualized attention (Schrum & Fitzgerald, 1996), creating a comfort zone (Norum,

TABLE 6.1 INCENTIVES AND OBSTACLES AFFECTING TECHNOLOGY ADOPTION AND INTEGRATION

Incentives

- Adequate equipment and resources (Becker, 1994; Fabry & Higgs, 1997; Hadley & Sheingold, 1993; Office of Technology Assessment, 1995; Topp, Mortenson, & Grandgenett, 1995)
- Supportive environment that allows "risk taking" (Becker, 1994; Topp, Mortenson, & Grandgenett, 1995, p. 12; Willis, 1993)
- "Expectations and encouragement are vital to the infusion of technology into the educational process" (Topp, Mortenson, & Grandgenett, 1995, p. 13)
- Collegiality among users (e.g., teachers) (Becker, 1994)
- Smaller class sizes (Becker, 1994)
- "Exemplary teachers were in schools that had nearly twice as many computer-using teachers" (Becker, 1994, p. 303)
- Personal interest (Becker, 1994; Ertmer, et al., 1999)
- Extra time (Fabry & Higgs, 1997; Hadley & Sheingold, 1993)
- Staff development and support (Becker, 1994; Fabry & Higgs, 1997; Office of Technology Assessment, 1995; Willis, 1993)
- "Exemplary teachers simply had higher standards and greater perceived needs than did the other computer users." (Becker, 1994, p. 315)
- Motivated to make lessons more interesting (Ertmer, et al., 1999)
- Preparing students for the future. (Ertmer, et al., 1999)
- Empowering teachers (Fabry & Higgs, 1997, p. 390)

Obstacles

- Lack of technology skills and knowledge (Martinez & Woods, 1995)
- Lack of equipment (Ertmer, et al., 1999)
- Mismatch with classroom style (Ertmer, et al., 1999)
- Lack of staff development (Ertmer, et al., 1999; Fabry & Higgs, 1997; Office of Technology Assessment, 1995; Topp, Mortenson, & Grandgenett, 1995)
- Absence of incentive or improper incentives (Martinez & Woods, 1995)
- Absence of environmental support (Martinez & Woods, 1995)
- Lack of motivation (Martinez & Woods, 1995)
- Lack of equipment (Ertmer, et al., 1999)
- Lack of time (Ertmer, et al., 1999; Office of Technology Assessment, 1995)
- Lack of relevance (Ertmer, et al., 1999)
- Lack of confidence (Ertmer, et al., 1999)
- Lack of funding (Fabry & Higgs, 1997; Office of Technology Assessment, 1995)
- Lack of access (Fabry & Higgs, 1997; Office of Technology Assessment, 1995)
- "Innate dislike for change (especially change mandated from above) is the most basic and significant barrier to technology integration." (Fabry & Higgs, 1997, p. 388)
- "Top down projects tend to fail over time." (Willis, 1993, p. 29)
- Current assessment practices (Office of Technology Assessment, 1995)

(Adapted, with permission, from Sugar, 2002, p. 13)

1997), and other similar factors. Fullan and Stiegelbauer (1991) noted that "nothing has promised so much and has been so frustratingly wasteful as the thousands of workshops and conferences that led to no significant change in practice when the teachers return to their classrooms" (p. 315). Determining the obstacles that impede teachers from using technology and factors that motivate teachers' beliefs about integrating technology is critical in order to implement fundamental and continual changes in the classroom.

Peg Ertmer (Ertmer, 1999; Ertmer, et al., 1999) distinguishes between these two obstacles as being first-order barriers and second-order barriers to technology. First-order barriers are external to the particular environment, whereas second-order barriers are internal to the school setting. Second-order barriers "confront fundamental beliefs about current practice, thus leading to new goals, structures or roles" (Ertmer, 1999, p. 48). Both of these types of obstacles are prevalent in adopting new technologies. Teacher-Leader/Designers need to confront both types of barriers simultaneously during the adoption process (Ertmer, 1999; Ertmer, et al., 1999, p. 70). There is a distinct interplay between these first-order and second-order barriers. Ertmer and colleagues (1999) noted that "researchers have suggested that teachers' beliefs about the role of technology in the classroom may either reduce or magnify the effects of first-order barriers" (p. 55), and that "second-order barriers may persist even when first-order barriers are removed" (p. 70). These intrinsic barriers toward technology are indefatigable because teachers' fundamental beliefs toward technology are more difficult to modify. Thus, we encourage Teacher-Leader/Designers to be open in adopting new technologies. A willingness to change one's attitude toward using new technologies is imperative. The Office of Technology Assessment (1995) found that "many technology-rich sites continue to struggle with how to integrate technology into the curriculum" (p. 30). Concentrating on shaping teachers' beliefs about using technology and removing these second-order beliefs are critical variables during a technology adoption and integration process.

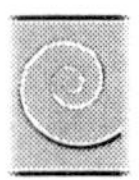

THE PROCESS OF ADOPTING INNOVATIONS

An effective way of adopting new technologies is to heed lessons learned from Everett Rogers' (2003) work with diffusion of innovations. Rogers studied how individuals adopted new technologies (i.e., set of knowledge), such as innovative agricultural techniques. Teacher-Leader/Designers can learn from Rogers' experiences and research. Our assumption to understand, learn, and eventually use new technologies is quite similar to Rogers' research on how one adopts innovations. In fact, when Teacher-Leader/Designers become aware of, learn, and eventually use a new technology (e.g., streaming video) in their classrooms, they are indeed adopting an innovation. Being cognizant of these factors will help Teacher-Leader/Designers become effective technology users.

Rogers stated that there are five distinct stages of adopting innovations: *Knowledge, Persuasion, Decision, Implementation,* and *Confirmation.* A description of each of these stages follows.

- *Knowledge*

  The focal point of this initial stage is the specific knowledge or skill that is associated with the particular innovation. For example, to understand how to create digital videos, one's concentration would be focused on all of the skills that are necessary to create a basic digital video. Adopters are not ready to use the proposed innovation, but would like to become aware of it. Particular features (e.g., editing Quicktime movies of student projects) of an innovation and an introduction of the innovation need to be communicated.
- *Persuasion*

  After gaining knowledge about the innovation and its particular features, new users are not only ready to gain more information, but they can be influenced about adopting this innovation. After going through the *Knowledge* stage, they will become increasingly curious about the new product or idea. During this stage, it is important that essential information is given about the innovation in order to persuade adopters to make a decision. The goal of this information is intended to have users interact and discuss the merits of the proposed innovation and form a positive impression of it. At the end of this stage, users hopefully can support the adoption of this innovation.
- *Decision*

  After proceeding through the first two adoption stages, users are now ready to "see" or visualize the particular innovation. If users have made the decision to "see" your proposed innovation, then it is the appropriate time to actually demonstrate the various features and the actual innovation. Note that users probably need to have positive support (established in the *Persuasion* stage) before a decision is made. During the demonstration, users can be encouraged to try the innovation to help their adoption decision.
- *Implementation*

  If users have successfully learned the first three Adoption stages, they are now ready to learn about the innovation. The overall intention is to try and start using the innovation. At this stage, it is imperative to provide the necessary and effective training to support this use and provide additional information about the innovation, if necessary.
- *Confirmation*

  After going through a successful *Implementation* stage, individuals will become regular and consistent users of the innovation. Essentially, they have confirmed that they indeed have adopted this innovation. Users will recognize the benefits of using the particular innovation and will integrate its use in their daily life. In fact, users at the *Confirmation* stage may want to convince others to use a particular innovation and thus become an advocate. These individuals should start at the *Knowledge* stage with new users in order to help continue the new adoption process.

In addition to these adoption stages, Everett Rogers has identified five types of individuals based on how they adopt innovations. He distinguishes these types as adopters and resisters. Adopters are more likely to accept and adopt innovations, whereas resisters oppose change and innovations. The five types of adopters are:

- *Innovators:* These individuals are very eager to try out new ideas; they are rash, risk-takers, and dangerous when trying out innovations or innovative practices.
- *Early adopters:* These individuals are respectable and have the greatest degree of opinion leadership in most communities. Potential adopters look to early adopters for advice. Early adopters are the individuals to check with before testing a new idea and when one is at the *Knowledge* stage.
- *Early majority:* These individuals are deliberate and will usually adopt new ideas right before the average adopter. They may consider and discuss ideas with their peers before entering the two *Decision* and *Implementation* stages and completely adopting a new idea.
- *Late majority:* These individuals are naturally skeptical. The decision to adopt the proposed innovation may be both an economic necessity and a response to increasing pressures from peers and the community. Late majority individuals can be influenced by early majority individuals. They disregard the adoption practices of Innovators and Early Adopters, because they perceive the latter two groups as being risky and too novel. However, if they observe early majority colleagues embracing an innovation, then they may not be as skeptical.
- *Laggards:* These individuals are usually traditional and are the ultimate resisters. Their decisions often are based on what has been done in the past. These individuals interact primarily with others who also have relatively traditional values and probably are not influenced by the other types of adopters.

Regarding Rogers' specific adoption stages and types of adopters, the next question is what does this information mean for you as a teacher and, more important, as a Teacher-Leader/Designer? For example, according to Rogers' categories, what kind of adopter are you? Are you always the first one to try something new, or are you initially skeptical about trying out a new "fad?" What kind of adopters are your colleagues? Are any of your colleagues laggards who resist any change that is proposed? What kind of adopter is your principal? Does she tend to resist change, fully embrace it, or is she somewhere in the middle? As a Teacher-Leader/Designer, not only can you become aware of your own practices, but you can also be proactive in helping others with this adoption process.

Rogers (1995) observed:

> Getting a new idea adopted, even when it has obvious advantages, is often very difficult. Many innovations require a lengthy period, often of many years, from the time they become available to the time they are widely adopted. Therefore, a common problem for many individuals and organizations is how to speed up the rate of diffusion of an innovation. (p. 1)

There are several restraining forces that inhibit the successful adoption of innovations in schools. The existing school structure and the community, as well as the corresponding decision-making process, can either promote or prevent the adoption process. The unstable nature of technology and possible misconceptions about technology (e.g., instructional media vs. instructional technology; soft technology vs. hard technology) also play a critical role in the acceptance of new technologies. Teacher-Leader/Designers can offer guidance on how to accept and embrace innovation and new technologies. This guidance might include the following steps. It is important for Teacher-Leader/Designers to communicate that in order for an innovation to take hold, it must be accepted, implemented, and maintained. To complete these three activities, one should follow the five Adoption stages and not force or skip a particular stage. For example, one should not ask teachers to *decide* about a new technology until they complete the *Knowledge* and *Persuasion* stages. Teachers should not be trained on a new technology until they have completed the first three stages and have entered the *Implementation* phase.

Other methods that encourage the adoption of an innovation are described by Rogers (1995) and include the following four techniques:

- *Relative advantage:* The degree to which an innovation is perceived as being better than the idea it supersedes." (p. 212)
- *Compatability:* The degree to which an innovation is perceived as consistent with the existing values, past experiences, and needs of potential adopters.
- *Complexity:* The degree to which an innovation is perceived as relatively difficult to understand and use (p. 242)
- *Observability:* The degree to which the results of an innovation are visible to others. (p. 244)

Rogers' identification of adoption stages, types of adopters, and strategies for adoption and implementation of innovations provide essential knowledge on how to incorporate technologies as a Teacher-Leader/Designer.

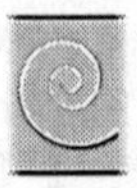

HOW TO MEASURE EFFECTIVE TECHNOLOGY

The existing literature lists numerous ways to evaluate effective technology use. The American Association of Colleges for Teacher Education (AACTE) has an Interactive Teacher Preparation School Technology and Readiness (STaR) program (AACTE, 2005). There are books that detail the selection and use of instructional media (Romiszowski, 1988) and existing formative and summative evaluation techniques that can be applied to the evaluation of instructional media and technology (Dick, Carey, & Carey, 2005). Overall, there are several factors to consider when evaluating instructional media and technology, including the actual task, learners, economic, technical, administrative, and physical factors. One must observe the instructional intent, its instructional techniques, and the actual effectiveness of the proposed instructional media and technology.

The following are specific criteria to consider when evaluating instructional media and technology.

- *Clarity:* Are the accompanying instructional materials clearly understandable to the instructors and students? Are the instructions and layout sensible and organized?
- *Impact:* Did the instruction have an impact on learner's attitudes and achievement of the specific objectives and goals?
- *Feasible:* Given the available resources (e.g., time, context), can learners complete the instruction within areas in a reasonable amount of time?
- *Instructional value:* Do the instructional media match the actual skills and competences to be taught? Do they match the curriculum and curricular goals?
- *Content:* Are the materials complete, accurate, and current?
- *Sound instructional techniques:* Are these techniques accurate and current? Will they arouse motivation and interest?
- *Design evaluation:* Evaluate the actual program's content as well as its screen layout (if any).
- *Economic factors:* These factors refer to practical constraints of affording instructional media. Are funds available for instructional media?
- *Learners' attitudes:* What is the impact of instruction on learners' attitudes and achievement of the objectives and goals?
- *Teacher and administrators' attitudes and skills:* The attitudes and skills of teachers and administrators must be considered. This is a critical variable in the overall acceptance of instructional media.
- *Physical environment:* This also is another critical variable to consider in evaluating and eventually adopting instructional media. Can the school's physical resources support the effective use of the proposed instructional media?

Awareness and utilization of these specific criteria for evaluating instructional media and technology is another required knowledge set for becoming a Teacher-Leader/Designer.

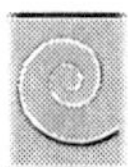

WHAT IS A TECHNOLOGY FACILITATOR?

A technology facilitator is an individual at either the school level or district level who supports teachers' technology use and integration. This job title may be a technology facilitator, technology coach, technology mentor, technology learning coordinator, or other similar designation. The technology facilitator's job is to provide technology support and guidance for teachers, school administrators, and students. Primary job responsibilities include troubleshooting problems with technological hardware, resolving technical problems that occur, and providing support for teachers and administrators in effectively instructing students in using an assortment of technologies.

Several research studies (Cole, Simkins, & Penul, 2002; Kariuki, Franklin, & Duran, 2001; Polselli, 2002; Smith, 2000; Smith & O'Bannon,

1999; Sprague, Kopfman, & de Levante Dorsey, 1998; Sugar, in press; Swan, et al., 2002) have focused on the benefits of having a technology facilitator. Similar to the concept of linking experienced teachers with novice teachers for professional development purposes (e.g., Anzul, 2000), a technology facilitator guides teachers in the use and integration of technology in their respective classrooms. The former take on several roles in this facilitator-teacher relationship, including "reviewer, director, monitor, facilitator, and evaluator" (Smith, 2000). Study results indicated that an overwhelming number of teachers benefit from a technology facilitator program (e.g., Polselli, 2002).

A technology facilitator role is found in various school districts across the nation. For example, the North Carolina Department of Public Instruction (2000) IMPACT Guidelines for Media and Technology programs recommend that:

> The school library media coordinator and the instructional technology facilitator work closely with teachers, administrators, students, and support personnel. All of these people must be involved in the planning, implementation, and evaluation of an instructional program infused with media and technology.

The International Society for Technology in Education (ISTE) and the National Council for Accreditation of Teacher Education (NCATE) have existing standards for Educational Technology Programs (ISTE, 2005). There are two types of standards: technology facilitation and technology leadership. Technology facilitators are trained to:

> Teach technology applications; demonstrate effective use of technology to support student learning of content; and provide professional development, mentoring, and basic technical assistance for other teachers who require support in their efforts to apply technology to support student learning. (ISTE, 2005)

Technology leaders are prepared to become technology directors, coordinators, or specialists. They are responsible for the "computing systems, facilities planning and management, instructional program development, staff development, and other advanced applications of technology to support student learning (ISTE, 2005).

You likely have worked with or at least are aware of technology facilitators at your own school or district. We encourage you to develop effective ways of working with your technology facilitator. By developing your own Teacher-Leader/Designer skills, we anticipate that you will develop and maintain a successful relationship with technology facilitators and leaders.

WAYS TO IMPROVE YOUR TECHNOLOGY SKILLS

With the increasing amount of new instructional media available most teachers will probably wish to become better technology users. There are several ways to enhance these skills, such as attending professional development sessions, working with a technology facilitator, attending continuing education courses, and other appropriate means. Because there is a natural tendency for Teacher-Leader/Designers to improve their teaching skills, we anticipate that learning new technologies will be a continual process in your classrooms. We recommend that you become cognizant of your own instructional media and technology needs and your own adoption tendencies, and become an advocate and supporter of technology use for other teachers and school administrators.

WHY IS EFFECTIVE TECHNOLOGY IMPORTANT?

We speculate that if this book had been written in the twentieth century (i.e., before 1985), some teachers, school administrators and other stakeholders would question the need for students to use technology in the classroom. Perhaps others would agree on the need for technology in the classroom, but it would be considered supplementary to the core disciplines. Since the advent and abundance of personal technologies (e.g., personal computers, the Internet, DVDs), much of teachers' professional careers and students' future employment opportunities involve technology. Few teachers, school administrators, parents, school board members, and other stakeholders would disagree with this statement and would embrace the inclusion of technology in all core curricula. Instructional media and instructional technology (i.e., hard and soft technologies) are the essential tools of a successful Teacher-Leader/Designer. Without adequate knowledge and actual resources, it will be difficult for teachers to design quality lessons and take on leadership roles within their schools. Understanding how incentives and obstacles are associated with technology use, how the adoption of innovations occur, how technology is measured, and how the role of a technology facilitator will help support and sustain the effective use of technology for Teacher-Leader/Designers.

SUMMARY

A Teacher-Leader/Designer should possess effective technology skills. Teacher-Leader/Designers continually use both instructional media and instructional technology to remain successful and to facilitate students' learning. Factors such as understanding the relationship between instructional media and instructional methods, the factors that influence the use of instructional technology, the adoption of innovations, the measurement of effective technology use, and the role of a technology facilitator all are essential to being a technology advocate and a frequent technology user. By embracing the necessary technology skills, Teacher-Leader/Designers will remain influential and be successful in their schools.

CASE STUDY

Bob Mason, principal at J. Rosemont High School, reviewed his recent e-mail messages and reviewed a list of professional development activities that have occurred at Rosemont for over a three-year period. These activities included workshop evaluation forms, a descriptive listing of workshop topics, a listing of Rosemont teachers and staff members who attended, and other relevant documents. Mr. Mason was preparing for his meeting with Monica LeBere, one of the technology facilitators in the school districts. Apparently, there have been "issues" with LeBere's workshops and Rosemont teachers. Even when there was consistent attendance among Rosemont teachers (usually five or more teachers attend these workshops), the teachers (and subsequently their students) were not using the new technology that was purchased with state funding. Mr. Mason has always adopted the "build it and they will come" mentality. During the past four years, he actively purchased the most current technologies, such as SmartBoards, CPS remote access system, Inspiration, and others. Superintendent Kester commented that Mr. Mason is willing to try anything and will help his staff overcome any issues with resources and funding. However, he noted that Rosemont's test scores essentially were the same as the other high schools in the district. Also, Rosemont teachers recently completed a technology use survey and a majority admitted that they were not "regular users" of several technologies that Mason had purchased. When Mr. Mason questioned Ms. LeBere about the survey results, she said all of the teachers were "laggards." What questions should Mr. Mason ask Ms. LeBere concerning this issue? Using Rogers' adoption stage and adopter type criteria, critique this situation. Why are teachers resisting Ms. LeBere's efforts in helping them over these technology obstacles?

ACTIVITIES

1. Create a technology inventory. List your past and current technology needs. Identify how you met your past technology needs. Speculate how you can learn your current technology needs. Were you successful in meeting your previous technology needs? What are some ways to help acquire your current technology needs?

2. Interview a technology facilitator from your school or your school district. Find out what this individual does during a typical school day. How would you rate the value of having a technology facilitator working with teachers? How many roles does this individual have? Rate this individual's leadership skills within your school and district.

3. Interview three teachers and your principal about their use of technologies. How do they define instructional media and instructional technology? What are the best ways for these individuals to adopt new technologies? Compare similarities and differences with your own responses.

DISCUSSION QUESTIONS

1. Your principal recently commented, "Technology *always* will improve schools and student learning." How would you react to this statement? Do you agree or disagree?

2. Review Rogers' adopter categories. What kind of adopter are you? Explain and illustrate your type. Explain any conflicts that you may have with your fellow teachers and school administrators.

3. What are the best ways for you to adopt new technologies? Describe and illustrate these best practices.

REFERENCES

American Association of Colleges for Teacher Education. (2005). *Teacher prep STaR chart.* Retrieved April 11, 2005, from http://star.aacte.org/.

Anzul, J. (2000). Teacher team develops a district mentoring program. *Kappa Delta Pi Record, 36*(2), 65–67.

Becker, H. (1994). How exemplary computer-using teachers differ from other teachers: Implications for realizing the potential of computers in schools. *Journal of Research on Computing in Education, 26*(3), 291–321.

Cole, K., Simkins, M. & Penul, W. (2002). Learning to teach with technology: Strategies for inservice professional development. *Journal of Technology and Teacher Education, 10*(3), 431–455.

Cuban, L. (1986). *Teachers and Machines: The Classroom Use of Technology Since 1920.* New York: Teachers' College Press.

Dale, E. (1969). *Audiovisual Methods in Teaching.* (3rd ed.). New York: Dryden.

Dick, W., Carey, L., & Carey, J. (2005). *The systematic design of instruction.* (6th ed.). Boston: Allyn & Bacon.

Ely, D. (1963). *The Changing Role of the Audiovisual Process in Education: A Definition and a Glossary of Related Terms.* Washington, D.C.: National Education Association.

Ertmer, P. (1999). Addressing first- and second-order barriers to change: Strategies for technology integration. *Educational Technology Research and Development, 47*(4), 47–61.

Ertmer, P., Addison, P., Lane, M., Ross, E., & Woods, D. (1999). Examining teachers' beliefs about the role of technology in the elementary classroom. *Journal of Research on Computing in Education, 32*(1), 54–72.

Fabry, D., & Higgs, J. (1997). Barriers to the effective use of technology in education: Current status. *Journal of Educational Computing Research, 17*(4), 385–395.

Fullan, M., & Stiegelbauer, S. (1991). *The new meaning of educational change.* (2nd ed.). New York: Teachers College Press.

Hadley, M., & Sheingold, K. (1993). Commonalities and distinctive patterns in teachers' integration of computers. *American Journal of Education, 101*(3), 261–315.

Heinich, R., Molenda, M., Russell, J. D., & Smaldino, S. E. (2001). *Instructional Media and Technologies for Learning.* (7th ed.). Englewood Cliffs, NJ:Prentice-Hall.

International Society for Technology in Education. (2005). *NCATE standards for educational technology programs.* Retrieved April 8, 2005, from http://cnets.iste.org/ncate/index.html.

Kariuki, M., Franklin, T., & Duran, M. (2001). A technology partnership: Lessons learned by mentors. *Journal of Technology and Teacher Education, 9*(3), 407–417.

Martinez, J., & Woods, M. (1995). The value and planned use of educational technology in higher education: Results of a faculty service needs assessment. *College & University Media Review, 2*(1), 25–38.

North Carolina Department of Public Instruction. (2000). *IMPACT guidelines for media and technology program.* Retrieved July 15, 2004, from http://www.ncwiseowl.org/Impact/Introduction.htm.

Office of Technology Assessment. (1995). *Teachers and Technology: Making the Connection.* Washington, D.C.: US Government Printing Office.

Oxford University Press. (2002). *Shorter Oxford English Dictionary on Historical Principles.* (5th ed.). New York: Oxford University Press.

Polselli, R. (2002). Combining web-based training and mentorship to improve technology integration in the K–12 classroom. *Journal of Technology and Teacher Education, 10*(2), 247–272.

Reigeluth, C. M. (1996). A new paradigm of ISD? *Educational Technology, 36*(3), 13–20.

Rogers, E. (1995). *Diffusion of Innovations.* (4th ed.). New York: Free Press.

Rogers, E. M. (2003). *Diffusion of Innovations.* (5th ed.). New York: Free Press.

Romiszowski, A. J. (1988). *The Selection and Use of Instructional Media for Improved Classroom Teaching and For Interactive, Individualized Instruction.* London: Kogan Page.

Schrum, L., & Fitzgerald, M. (1996). A challenge for the information age: Educators and the Internet. *International Journal of Educational Telecommunications,* 2(2/3), 107–120.

Smith, S. (2000). Graduate students mentor for technology success. *Teacher Education and Special Education, 23*(2), 167–182.

Smith S., & O'Bannon, B. (1999). Faculty members infusing technology across teacher education: A mentorship model. *Teacher Education and Special Education, 22*(2), 123–135.

Sprague, D., Kopfman, K., & de Levante Dorsey, S. (Winter, 1998). Faculty development in the integration of technology in teacher education courses. *Journal of Computing in Teacher Education, 14*(2), 24–28.

Sugar, W. (2002). Applying human-centered design to technology integration: Three alternative technology perspectives. *Journal of Computing in Teacher Education, 19*(1), 12–17.

Sugar, W. (in press). Instructional technologist as a coach: Impact of a situated professional development program on teachers' technology use. *Journal of Technology and Teacher Education.*

Swan, K., Holmes, A., Vargas, J., Jennings, S., Meier, E., & Rubenfeld, L. (2002). Situated professional development and technology integration: The capital area technology and inquiry in education (CATIE) mentoring program. *Journal of Technology and Teacher Education, 10*(2), 169–190.

Topp, N., Mortenson, R. & Grandgenett, N. (1995). Building a technology-using faculty to facilitate technology-using teachers. *Journal of Computing in Teacher Education, 11*(3), 11–14.

Willis, J. (1993). What conditions encourage technology use? It depends on the context. *Computers in the Schools, 9*(4), 13–32.

Chapter 7

Effective Action Research Skills

This chapter will describe the importance of possessing and practicing action research skills and methods. It will define action research, describe the purpose of action research methodology, and discuss the origins of early action research practices. This chapter also will list four distinct action research phases and describe how a Teacher-Leader/Designer can implement pertinent activities within each of these four phases. Teacher-Leader/Designers will likely benefit from becoming active action researchers.

After reading this chapter, you will be able to:

1. Define research and action research.
2. Describe the main purposes of action research.
3. Describe the origins of action research.
4. List four distinct action research phases.
5. Discuss the relationship between a Teacher-Leader/Designer and action research.
6. Describe activities for each of the four action research phases.
7. Describe the importance of possessing action research skills.

WHAT IS ACTION RESEARCH?

Before we define and discuss the characteristics of action research, we must first answer the question, "What is research?" By conducting research, one addresses a problem that needs to be investigated through a process of inquiry. By going through this process, one provides "explanations that enable individuals to understand the nature of the problem" (Stringer, 1999). Tomal (2003) noted that research is a

> Systematic process of attempting to find a solution to a problem (when the solution is not known) using an acceptable methodology. [It is a] . . . careful undertaking to discover new facts and relationships concerning a solution that is unknown. (Johnson, 2005, p. 1)

Research is also a process of "seeing, a procedure used to view and re-view the world in order to understand it." It is "the systematic method used to collect data to answer questions" (Johnson, 2005). According to Charles (1988), "Research is an undertaking that people initiate and follow through on in a more or less self-directed way. It is a process of inquiry, of finding answers to important questions." Essentially, there are two main categories of research methodologies: quantitative and qualitative. There are several books that describe the differences between a quantitative research methodology and a qualitative research methodology (e.g., Patton, 2002).

What exactly is action research? Action research primarily employs qualitative research methods that are used to understand problems in school settings and organizations. Action research provides an understanding and analysis of individuals' discourse, relevant activities, and social relationships within an organization (Kemmis & McTaggart, 1988). By applying specific action research methods, one can observe problems from the perceptions of practitioners within particular contexts and evaluate possible interventions aimed at improving a particular practice (Argyis & Schön, 1989). "In action research, a researcher works with a group to define a problem, collect data to determine whether or not this is indeed the problem, then experiment with potential solutions to the problem" (Brooks & Watkins, 1994).

Several books and existing resources have promoted action research principles for practicing teachers (e.g., Johnson, 2005; Mills, 2000; Sagor, 2005; Stringer, 2004; Tomal, 2003). Tomal (2003) described action research as a "systematic process of solving educational problems and making improvements." Mills (2000) states that action research is a systematic inquiry that enables teachers to "gather information about the ways that their particular schools operate, how they teach, and how well their students learn." According to Sagor (2005), action research is a "a disciplined process of inquiry conducted by and for those taking the action. The primary reason for engaging in action research is to assist the actor in improving or refining his or her actions." Action research also is "the process of studying a real school or classroom situation to understand and improve the quality of actions or instruction" (Johnson, 2005). It is conducted in a "systematic and orderly way for teachers to observe their practice or to explore a problem and a possible course of action" (Johnson, 2005).

THE PURPOSE OF ACTION RESEARCH

In reviewing these various action research definitions, there are three explicit characteristics that are common among each definition, including:

- *Systematic:* When one conducts an action research project, one must complete specific activities in a systematic or disciplined approach. Although there are a variety of methods to employ for an action research project (see Four Distinct Action Research Phases below), one must complete a project in an orderly and documented manner.
- *Problem-solving:* The intent of an action research project is to solve a particular problem or a set of related problems. To complete this task, one collects data related to a particular issue and problem.
- *Improvements:* After collecting information on a particular issue, one makes recommendations or "takes action" to improve the current problem or a set of related problems. The main output of an action research project is an action plan. The intent of this plan is focused on improving the current situation or defined problem.

The overall purpose of initiating and implementing an action research project is to solve a specific problem in a systematic manner with the intent of making improvements. Teachers who conduct action research projects "explicitly and purposefully become part of the change process by engaging the people in the organization by studying their own problems in order to solve these problems" (Patton, 2002). Action research participants must be "committed to continued professional development and school improvement" (Mills, 2000). Action research projects are most effective and relevant when they are contextualized within a local environment. These projects empower teachers to be able to analyze and evaluate the existing school structure and culture.

Several action research proponents advocate that action research mindset enables teachers to enhance their everyday work practices by reviewing their respective goals and procedures, their effectiveness, and their planning activities and strategies (Stringer, 1999). Action research projects can affect curriculum development, classroom processes, existing school management practices, and other relevant activities. Action research projects also engage teachers into a reflective practice. These projects help teachers gain insight by developing a reflective practice that affects positive changes in the school environment and improves student outcomes (Mills, 2000). By developing their own reflective practice through their respective action research projects, teachers are engaged in the development of a learning community in their respective schools. (For more information on these learning communities, see Chapter 10).

THE ORIGINS OF ACTION RESEARCH

Informal action research practices can be traced to existing research practices conducted several hundred years ago, but the concept of action research was formalized in the mid-1940s. The formation of the action research discipline can be attributed to Kurt Lewin, Stephen Kemmis, Robin McTaggart, Peter Checkland, and others.

Several action research proponents recognize Kurt Lewin as the "father of action research." Following World War II, Lewin recognized a new stage in the development of social sciences research. In order to observe and examine the dynamic problems social structures, he proposed the development of new instruments and techniques of social research (Lewin, 1946). He sought to study "quasi-stationary social equilibria and social changes" (Lewin, 1946). Features of Lewin's action research model included the following qualities: problem-driven; challenging the status quo; producing empirically disconfirmable propositions that could be systematically interrelated into a theory designed to be usable in everyday life (Lewin, 1946).

Because of his untimely death, Lewin never was able to fully develop a working action research model. However, other action research proponents extended his ideas, including Stephen Kemmis, Robin McTaggart, and Peter Checkland. Kemmis & McTaggart (1988) developed a "self reflective collaborative enquiry" focused on "social situations in order to improve rationality and justice of their own practices as well as their understanding of these practices and the situations in which these practices are carried out." They noted that "action research is a form of collective self-reflective enquiry undertaken by participants in social situations in order to improve the rationality and justice of their own social or educational practices" (Kemmis & McTaggart, 1988).

Checkland and associates developed a particular action research methodology labeled *Soft Systems Methodology.* By implementing *Soft Systems Methodology,* one examines:

> . . . human activity systems carried out through the process of attempting to solve problems. Its core is the idea that the researcher does not remain an observer outside the subject of investigation but becomes a participant in the relevant human group. (Checkland, 1981)

In defining human activity systems as a system of activities within a social system, one uses *Soft Systems Methodology* to understand "messy, real-world problems." This methodology is a structured way of thinking that focuses on a real-world situation that is perceived as problematical, with the aim of bringing about improvements in the situation (Checkland & Scholes, 1990). Several researchers currently are applying Checkland's *Soft Systems Methodology* to understanding "messy" problems in social settings.

WHAT IS THE RELATIONSHIP BETWEEN EDUCATIONAL RESEARCH AND ACTION RESEARCH?

There is a strong interrelationship between the goals of educational research and action research. Several action research proponents advocate the application of such principles in researching issues in educational settings. Tomal (2003) endorses action research as "one of the most practical and efficient methods of conducting research by educators." He comments that action research is a "viable approach for conducting meaningful and practical research for school improvement." The results of an action research report and its corresponding recommendations have the "potential to be a powerful agent of educational change" (Mills, 2000). Teachers are encouraged to use action research practices as part of their daily teaching practices (Mills, 2000). Seemingly, it is wise to employ and apply action research methods and principles to examine and to make sense of phenomenon occurring in educational settings.

FOUR DISTINCT ACTION RESEARCH PHASES

Although there is no consensus on a specific amount of phases, we have determined that there are four distinct action research phases (see Figure 7.1).

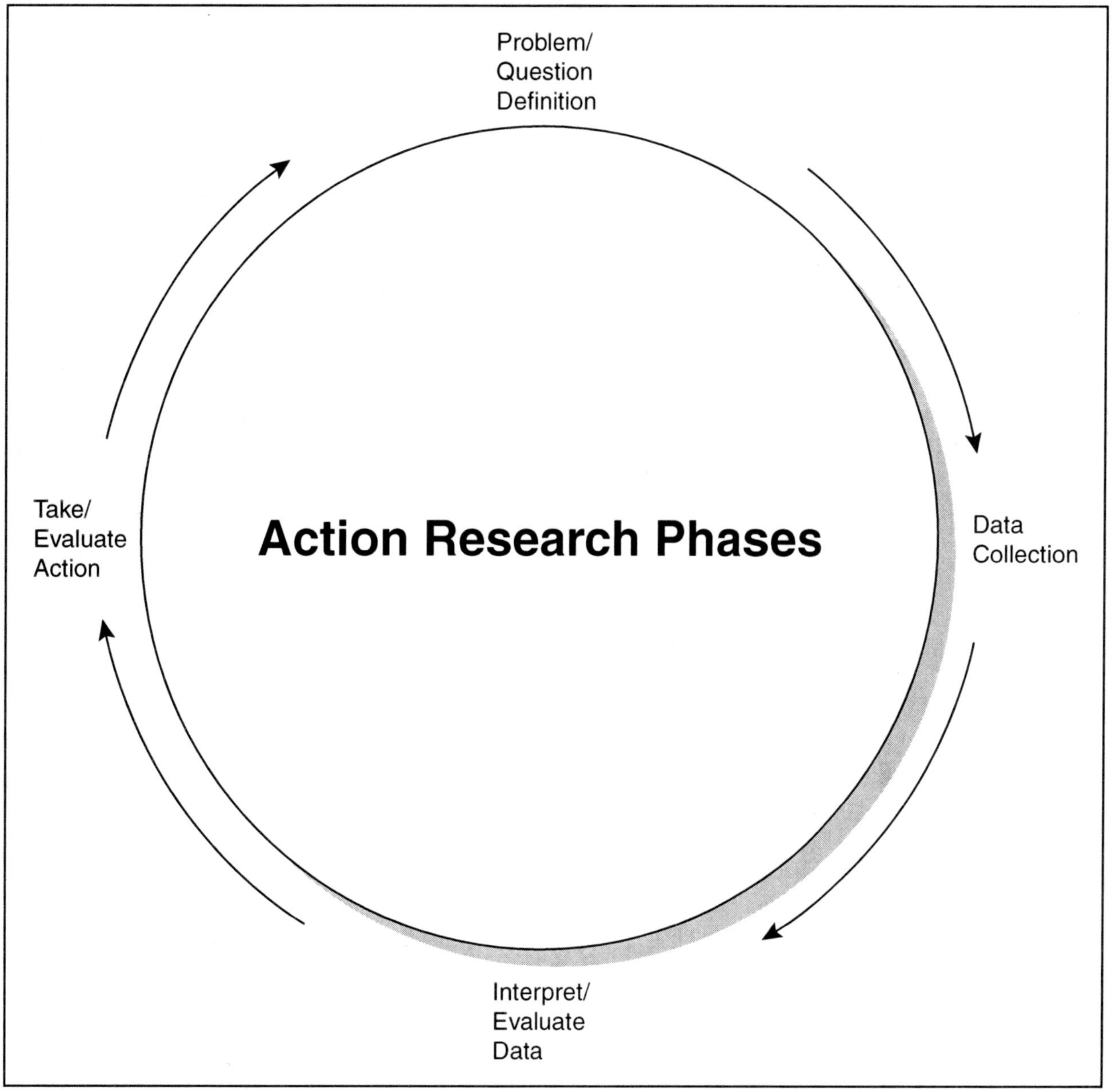

Figure 7.1 Four action research phases.

We formulated these phases based on several sources (i.e., Johnson, 2005; Mills, 2000; Sagor, 2005; Stringer, 2004; Tomal, 2003). These four phases include the following:

- *Problem/Question Definition:* During this first phase, one develops a problem statement and identifies an area of focus. One attempts to diagnose and resolve a particular issue. This issue may be a question that needs to be answered or a current topic that is problematic.
- *Data Collection:* After identifying a particular topic, one plans and collects information focused on answering and solving a particular problem.
- *Interpret/Evaluate Data:* After collecting data, one attempts to make sense of them. One interprets whether the data answer the specific question or problem. One also evaluates whether one can make recommendations based upon the information that was collected.
- *Take/Evaluate Action:* During this last phase, the focus of an action research project is realized. That is, after collecting, interpreting, and evaluating relevant data, one takes "action" and makes specific recommendations. Typically, one develops and initiates an action plan that either answers the original question or resolves the current problem. After this implementation, one evaluates the efficacy of this particular action plan.

One universal aspect of all action research models and corresponding phases is their recursive nature. Each phase builds upon itself. Also, one does not complete only one cycle of the four action research phases; one can complete multiple iterations. That is, after developing and evaluating an action plan during the *Take/Evaluate Action* phase, one can attempt to answer another question or investigate another problem in the next *Problem/Question Definition* phase. This recursive nature is effectively illustrated in Stringer's (2004) Action Research helix, or *The Look-Think-Act Research Cycle* (see Figure 7.2).

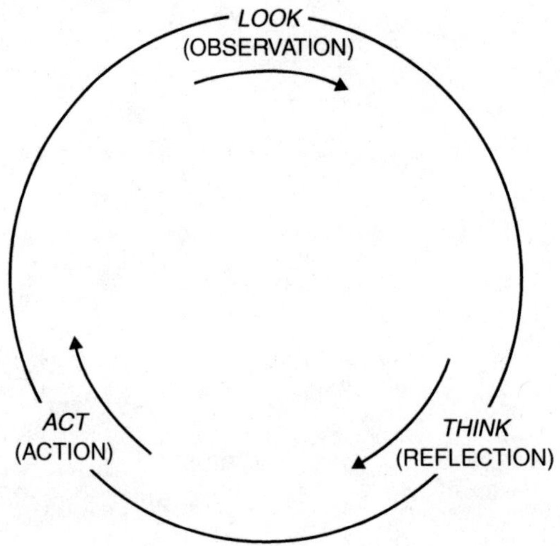

Figure 7.2 The Look-Think-Act Research Cycle.

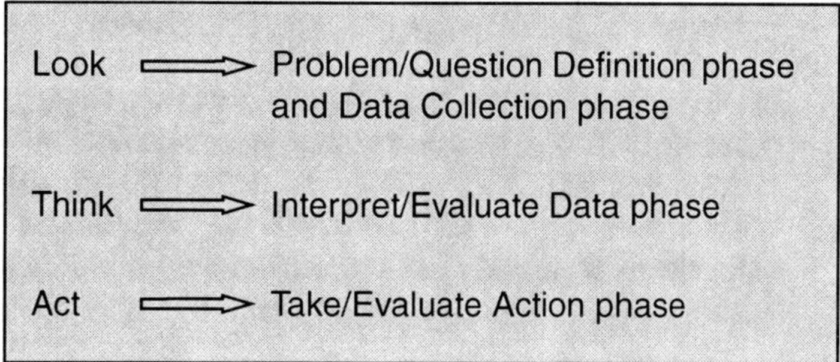

Figure 7.3 Relationship between Stringer's (2004) Look-Think-Act Research Cycle and the four action research phases.

First, one "looks" and observes during the *Problem/Question Definition* phase and the *Data Collection* phase. Then an action researcher "thinks" and reflects during the *Interpret/Evaluate Data* phase. Finally, one "acts" and takes action during the *Take/Evaluate Action* phase (see Figure 7.3). An action research project can continually go through these three phases.

WHAT IS THE RELATIONSHIP BETWEEN A TEACHER-LEADER/DESIGNER AND ACTION RESEARCH?

Knowledge and hands-on experience of action research principles and activities are essential for the Teacher-Leader/Designer. In fact, we are advocates of teachers becoming Teacher-Researchers in their classrooms and school settings. There is one main difference between a Teacher-Researcher and a Teacher-Leader/Designer. Action research is a skill that one should learn and adapt to one's own teaching practice. Teachers are not innate researchers. Novice teachers do not naturally go through the action research practices in their own classroom. However, teachers are innate leaders and innate designers. Both novice and experienced teachers clearly assume leadership roles in the classroom, and continually strive to design effective lesson plans for their students. Becoming an action researcher and acquiring the corresponding research skills will enhance and compliment the leadership and design skills of a Teacher-Leader/Designer.

HOW TO CONDUCT ACTION RESEARCH

Although there are numerous sources on how to conduct action research projects (e.g., Johnson, 2005; Mills, 2000; Sagor, 2005; Stringer, 2004; Tomal, 2003) and qualitative research methods (e.g., Patton, 2002), we offer the following information and advice on how to implement each of the four action research phases.

PROBLEM/QUESTION DEFINITION PHASE

During this phase, one must identify a problem or question to be answered. This problem or question should be current and within the local school setting. Mills (2000) recommends that the problem or question be within one's focus of control. The problem should have the potential to change or improve a situation and the action researcher should feel passionate about the content area.

DATA COLLECTION PHASE

During this phase, one must consider and identify various individuals (or stakeholders) who have a relationship to a particular project and who may have relevant information. These stakeholders may include teachers, principals, students, parents, school employees, and other pertinent individuals. Collect and obtain as much relevant information from such individuals. This information can be examples of students' current work, minutes from school board meetings, current school policies, and other relevant documents. Do your best to brainstorm possible information sources that you can obtain. If appropriate, involve your principal, fellow teachers, and other pertinent individuals in this process.

You can collect data from stakeholders through a variety of methods, including observations, individual or group interviews, existing data (e.g., school records), and note taking. Several action research proponents advise keeping a research journal. Coghlan & Brannick (2001) recommend that in each research journal entry, action researchers should write about a concrete experience that occurred during an observation; a reflection about the particular observation; a conceptualization that includes tentative conclusions, generalizations, and hypotheses; and tentative action items that can be included in the final action plan.

One of the critical elements of the data collection phase is *triangulation.* Triangulation refers to the ability to collect data from multiple sources (e.g., teachers, principal, students), instead of relying on one data source (e.g., one teacher). When action researchers triangulate, they also employ multiple methods (e.g., interviews, surveys, observations). If you establish your action research project and corresponding action plan on only one source and only use one method to collect this information, then your action research plan will be faulty and contain major deficiencies. When you conduct your action research project, collect data from multiple sources using multiple methods. Triangulating your data sources and methods will ensure that you perform an effective action research project and will subsequently have a valuable action plan.

INTERPRET/EVALUATE DATA PHASE

After you collect the necessary data, it is time to interpret and evaluate the results of your data collection. When you are collecting and evaluating your data, you need to be an impartial reporter or observer. Your job is to collect data, not influence the current phenomenon. You will code your data by identifying specific themes. We strongly recommend the use of constant comparison technique, as described by Glaser and Strauss (1967) and Lincoln and Guba (1985).

As described by Tomal (2003), an action researcher needs to see the entire picture and recognize hidden agendas. One should focus on the causes of the problem, not the obvious symptoms. An action researcher must not fall into the trap of the *faint hearted syndrome*, which is the fear that uncovering the inadequacies and blocks to reform to in an institution will unsettle the stability of the existing structure and culture.

TAKE/EVALUATE ACTION PHASE

This phase is the fun part, because this is where the action researcher takes action and makes specific recommendations. The impetus of an action research project is to scrutinize the current situation and institution. One should not shy away from making pertinent and potentially crucial recommendations. Collaboration among all relevant stakeholders during each of the four phases is critical.

Patton (2002) observed, "In action research, the process is the product." In your action plan, you should document your entire action research process. You will want to document these results, so your entire action research team and key stakeholders can react to these findings. Tomal (2003) recommends the following sections for an action plan: *Introduction and Problem Statement; Literature Review; Methods; Analysis;* and *Proposed Evaluation and Recommendations.* Concise descriptions of your action research process accompanied by ample illustrations will communicate your action research process and action research plan.

WHY ARE ACTION RESEARCH SKILLS IMPORTANT?

We believe that action research skills are essential ingredients of being a successful teacher. Possessing an action research mindset engages teachers in a constant, dynamic inquiry about their teaching and school culture. Although there may not be monetary incentives to participate in an action research project, there are tremendous benefits in initiating, examining, and implementing changes to one's work environment. We encourage Teacher-Leader/Designers to actively engage in action research projects in order to promote positive changes in their schools.

SUMMARY

We strongly recommend that Teacher-Leader/Designers learn and practice action research skills and related activities on a regular basis. Understanding the importance and nuances of the four action research phases is crucial to being an active action researcher. By providing a systematic, problem-solving approach with the intent of improving a current situation, Teacher-Leader/Designers are providing the leadership skills that are necessary for effective schools. We expect Teacher-Leader/Designers' action plans will prompt change and "action" in their respective schools. This activity will enable Teacher-Leader/Designers to become successful members of their school community.

CASE STUDY

Carol Benson is a third-grade teacher at Clinton Park Township Elementary School. She previously worked with developmentally disabled students at the first-, second-, and third-grade levels, but she was transferred to the regular third-grade curriculum four months ago. Prior to being a special education teacher, she was a first-grade teacher at Blooming Oaks Elementary for seven years. Both schools are in the same school district. After familiarizing herself with the third-grade curriculum and teaching twenty-seven third graders, Ms. Benson noticed a glaring deficiency in a majority of her students' math skills. Apparently, they could not grasp the concept of adding three multiple-digit numbers, and they could not "carry over" a number to the next digit (e.g., tens, hundreds). She recalled that this math skill was introduced in the first-grade curriculum and was regularly practiced in the second-grade curriculum. Carol consulted with her third-grade colleagues and found that they had observed the same deficiency. One of her colleagues, Mary Laurelson, suggested that their team conduct an action research project to examine why third graders could not perform this math task. The third-grade team plans to meet with the principal, Thomas Jimenez, next week to discuss this possibility. How can the third-grade team convince Mr. Jimenez of the benefits of conducting an action research project? If they obtain Mr. Jimenez's approval, how should the third-grade team plan their proposed action research project?

ACTIVITIES

1. For the next three weeks, plan a mini–action research project at your school. Go through each of the four action research phases in completing this project. Select a problem or question to explore. Describe how you would perform specific data collection activities and how you would triangulate them. Collect and interpret some data. Compose a preliminary action plan. After the three weeks, evaluate your action research project successes and failures. What will you do differently when you conduct your next action research project?

2. Review the four action research phases found in Figure 7.1. In your current teaching practice, identify activities that you already regularly perform in each of the phases. For example, do you already collect data on a regular basis to answer a question or solve a problem? Develop a plan on how you can increase the number of activities found in each of the four action research phases in the future. In your opinion, are teachers naturally Teacher-Researchers? Why or why not?

DISCUSSION QUESTIONS

1. What is your opinion of this statement: "Action research skills are one of the essential ingredients of being a successful teacher"? Are action research skills essential for being a successful teacher? What are the pros and cons of possessing action research skills?

2. Describe the relationship between a Teacher-Researcher and a Teacher-Leader/Designer from your own experiences as a teacher.

3. Peter Checkland wrote that the purpose of action research is to solve "messy, real-world problems." What "messy, real-world problems" can an action research project solve in your school setting?

REFERENCES

Argyris, C., & Schön, D. (1978) *Organizational Learning: A Theory of Action Perspective.* Reading, MA: Addison Wesley.

Brooks, A., & Watkins, K. E. (1994). *The Emerging Power of Action Inquiry Technologies.* San Francisco: Jossey-Bass.

Charles, C. M. (1988). *Introduction to Educational Research.* New York: Longman.

Checkland, P. B. (1981). *Systems Thinking, Systems Practice.* Chichester, UK: Wiley & Sons.

Checkland, P., & Scholes J. (1990). *Soft Systems Methodology in Action.* Chichester, UK: Wiley & Sons.

Coghlan, D., & Brannick, T. (2001). *Doing Action Research in Your Own Organization.* Thousand Oaks, CA: Sage.

Glaser, B. G., & Strauss, A. L. (1967). *The Discovery of Grounded Theory: Strategies for Qualitative Research.* Chicago: Aldine.

Johnson, A. P. (2005). *A Short Guide to Action Research.* (2nd ed.). Boston, MA: Pearson.

Kemmis, S., & McTaggart, R. (1988). *The Action Research Planner.* (3rd ed.). Geelong, Australia: Deakin University.

Lewin, K. (1946). Action research and minority problems. *Journal of Social Issues, 2,* 34–46.

Lincoln, Y., & Guba, E. (1985). *Naturalistic Inquiry.* Beverly Hills: Sage.

Mills, G. E. (2000). *Action Research: A Guide for the Teacher Researcher.* Upper Saddle River, NJ: Merrill.

Patton, M. Q. (2002). *Qualitative Research and Evaluation Methods.* Thousand Oaks, CA: Sage.

Sagor, R. (2005). *The Action Research Guidebook: A Four-Step Process for Educators and School Teams.* Thousand Oaks, CA: Corwin.

Stringer, E. T. (1999). *Action Research.* Thousand Oaks, CA: Sage.

Stringer, E. T. (2004). *Action Research in Education.* Upper Saddle River, NJ: Prentice-Hall.

Tomal, D. R. (2003). *Action Research for Educators.* Lanham, MD: Scarecrow.

Working with Each Other as Teacher-Leader/Designers

Mentoring New Teachers

This chapter will discuss the process of mentoring new teachers and why this is an important process for Teacher-Leader/Designers to be involved in. Mentoring new teachers is a natural role for Teacher-Leader/Designers to fulfill. As discussed in earlier chapters, Teacher-Leader/Designers are individuals within schools that have influence and the ability to conceive, design, and implement necessary elements for their school. Induction of new teachers is a critical component for the teaching profession to continue to grow and prosper. This induction process is best accomplished in a mentoring program.

After reading this chapter, you will be able to:

1. Define and describe a mentoring program for new teachers.
2. Articulate the need of mentoring programs for new teachers.
3. List and discuss the five phases experienced by first-year teachers.
4. Identify the five goals of most mentoring programs.
5. Describe the attributes of an effective mentor.
6. Describe the challenges of mentors.
7. List the responsibilities of the mentee.
8. Describe the expectations of the mentee.
9. Identify the desired outcomes of a mentoring program.

WHAT IS A MENTORING PROGRAM FOR NEW TEACHERS?

A mentoring program for teachers is an induction program designed to help beginning teachers become acclimated to a new school and become contributing, successful members of the teaching profession. The mentoring program is a process in which a skilled, experienced teacher (known as a mentor) is formally assigned a less-skilled and less-experienced teacher (known as a mentee) to serve as a role model, informer, listener, supporter, encourager, counselor, and friend. The overall objective for a mentoring program is to promote the professional development of new teachers.

The mentoring process is an ongoing, supportive relationship between the mentor and the mentee. According to Huling-Austin and Murphy (1987), "The assignment of a support teacher may well be the most powerful and cost-effective induction practice available to program developers" (pp. 35–36). Many studies (e.g., Halford, 1998; Lohr, 1999; Moir, 1999) support that beginning teachers benefit from mentoring programs because they are able to become successful teachers. "Mentor teachers have become known as occupational life savers for offering technical, social, and emotional support (Bey, 1995, p. 11). Mentoring is much like scaffolding: Initially the mentor's support is substantial, and gradually, with time and experience, more and more professional responsibilities are turned over to the mentee. As the mentee demonstrates increased professional competence and comprehension, the mentoring support is gradually withdrawn until it is no longer needed. Ultimately, the mentoring program is designed to help people learn and to support self-development.

WHY START A MENTORING PROGRAM?

A mentoring program for teachers is designed to help new teachers become successful professionals and to remain in the classroom. Approximately 30 percent of teachers leave the profession within the first five years of their teaching (Henke, Chen, Geis, & Knepper, 2000). In some areas of the country, the attrition rate of new teachers is even higher. This may be attributable, in part, to the erroneous belief that beginning teachers are fully prepared to successfully enter the profession without the help and support of veteran teachers (Villani, 1999). The first years, not to mention the first months, are critical for beginning teachers. Many new teachers believe they will be ready for teaching and will have less difficulty teaching than the "average" beginning teacher (Weinstein, 1988). However, most new teachers have a "reality shock" during their first year of teaching (Veenman, 1984). The following quote expresses how many teachers feel about their first year of teaching: "My descent from innocence was swift and brutal as a first-year teacher. I was completely overwhelmed in my classroom and had so many questions about what to do, how to do it, when to do it, and so on. I kept asking myself, 'What did I get myself into and where do I turn? Who can I turn to?'"

THE FIVE PHASES EXPERIENCED BY FIRST-YEAR TEACHERS

Ellen Moir (1999) has identified five phases that first-teachers experience during their first year of teaching. The first is the Anticipation Phase during which new teachers are idealistic, excited, and nervous. They are filled with anticipation and great hopes and expectations for their success in teaching their students. Second is the Survival Phase, which usually occurs during the first month of school. The beginning teacher is overwhelmed and simply wants to survive until the winter break. Third is the Disillusionment Phase, which typically occurs at the beginning of the third month when new teachers begin to question their commitment and competence in teaching. This is the time when their morale is at its lowest point. This is a very critical time period in the life of a new teacher. Fourth is the Rejuvenation Phase, a time when the new teachers' attitudes begin to rise. After winter break, teachers feel rested and rejuvenated. They return to school and their classrooms with renewed hope and a better understanding of how to manage their students more effectively. They are relieved that half of the school year is completed. The fifth and final phase is the Reflection, which occurs as the end of the year approaches. This is a time when teachers review their year and analyze what worked well and what did not. This phase is also a time of self-analysis.

As new teachers move through these phases during their first year of teaching, it is important that they have strong mentoring to help them deal effectively and rationally with each of these phases. Equally important, mentors need to be aware and anticipate the first-year phases of their mentees. This awareness and anticipation of the five phases beginning teachers will enter help mentors provide the necessary support that is needed by their mentees at that particular stage. In short, if the mentor is aware of the five phases that new teachers encounter, then they will be more likely to provide the appropriate guidance and support to help their mentee be successful during their first year.

IMPORTANT GOALS OF MENTORING PROGRAMS

A mentoring program is designed to help retain teachers in the profession. Teachers leave the classroom for many reasons, but research has found teachers who have effective mentors during their first year are more likely to remain in the teaching profession (Huling-Austin & Murphy, 1987). Mentoring programs help beginning teachers become competent and successful teachers. An effective mentoring program should include the following five goals (Huling-Austin, et al., 1989). The first goal of an effective mentoring program should be retaining teachers in the classroom. Beginning teachers benefit from meeting periodically with their mentors to emotionally release the many feelings and confusing thoughts they are experiencing during their first year of teaching. New teachers need to realize they are not alone; they have someone with whom to discuss their feelings of being overwhelmed, the uncertainties, and doubts about their competency as a teacher. Mentors can help beginning teachers put meaning into their teaching experiences, both inside and outside the classroom.

The second goal of an effective mentoring program should be improving teacher performance. Teaching is a practice and it is expected, with experience, for teachers to show improvement in their ability to teach effectively. This improvement will increase with experienced teachers helping the less-experienced teachers conquer the many issues and challenges that confront beginning teachers. Providing beginning teachers with helpful suggestions and insights will help boost their performance in the classroom.

The third goal is to help promote the personal and professional well-being of beginning teachers. For beginning teachers, the ability to withstand the pressures of first-year teaching require that they maintain a proper perspective in the classroom as well as in their personal life. Beginning teachers sometimes perceive a professional situation as a "life or death" catastrophe lacking a solution, when in reality a very logical solution exists. Mentors can help beginning teachers step back and examine challenges of the classroom in their proper context. Mentors can also encourage their mentees to maintain a healthy and balanced lifestyle by maintaining a nutrious diet, exercising on a regular basis, getting a proper amount of rest, as well as having outside interests other than teaching.

The fourth goal of an effective mentoring program helps beginning teachers in satisfying mandated requirements. All schools require teachers to meet specific mandates and requirements, often known as "paperwork." Each year, teachers state that the amount of paperwork to complete seems to increase. Helping beginning teachers wrestle the paperwork mountain into a manageable molehill is a substantial service that is often provided by mentors.

The fifth goal of an effective mentoring program is to help transmit the culture of the school. Newcomers appreciate having mentors teach them the school culture. "Mentors can alert newcomers to things that are not found written anywhere and might only learn about after they had inadvertently gone against the norm" (Villani, 2002, p. 10). All schools seem to have their own "way of doing things," and the sooner beginning teachers understand the school culture the more likely it is that they will avoid unnecessary problems.

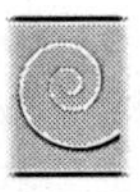

WHAT IS A MENTOR?

A mentor is a formal role assigned to an individual to help a less-skilled and less-experienced individual (in most cases, a beginning teacher). The purpose of a mentor is to promote the professional success of the mentee. Some of the major functions of a mentor are discussed below.

A mentor is a source of information. There are many things for a beginning teacher to learn. Often they do not know what they do not know, and if they did, they would not know where to seek answers. It is important that mentors provide the necessary information to their mentees in a timely manner. A mentor should help their mentee avoid saying, "No one ever told me I needed to know that!"

Serving as a sounding board and role-model is an important role of a mentor in initiating the mentee to the teaching profession. It is important that mentees trust their mentors; they should feel free to express their true feelings and concerns about professional issues they are dealing with. A mentor who is a good listener is typically highly valued by their mentee.

Mentors should be cheerleaders for their mentees. Beginning teachers can be overwhelmed, lonely, frustrated, stressed, and doubtful of their professional competency throughout their first year of teaching. Encouragement and praise from a mentor make a significant difference in how beginning teachers view themselves. It is important for beginning teachers to acknowledge and focus on their successes, not their failures. Mentors can help mentees achieve this.

CHARACTERISTICS OF A MENTOR

Successful mentors are experienced teachers who mentor for altruistic reasons. Mentors should possess a healthy self-concept and not be afraid to allow mentees to enter their "worlds." Mentors' classroom experience adds to their credibility. Current classroom teachers often have the highest credibility because they are dealing with the day-to-day reality of teaching.

Mentors should possess strong interpersonal skills. It is important that mentors can establish trusting and supporting relationships with others, especially with their mentees. Mentees should want to spend time with their mentor and feel comfortable going to them for any reason. Mentors must be excellent communicators. They must be able to clearly articulate the messages conveyed to their mentee. Of course, being a great communicator means being an active listener. Mentors should also be effective managers with good organizational skills. As stated earlier, mentors must always model appropriate behavior for their mentee, and organization is an important aspect of being an effective and successful teacher. Leadership skills and the ability to adapt to different needs and personalities of individuals are also important (Gordon, 1990).

Successful mentors find they receive as much as they give. Mentors often gain much from their mentoring experiences. "Not only do teachers find that they learn more about their own teaching as they convey what they know to new teachers, they also find that peer coaching enables them to go deeper into their own practice" (Villani, 2002, p. 5). Mentors need to articulate their professional beliefs and how these beliefs drive their decision-making and actions in the classroom. It is not unusual for the mentor to learn new teaching ideas or strategies from their mentee. Mentees are recent graduates of a university education program, and often possesses knowledge of the newest and latest teaching pedagogy. Thus, learning about best teaching practices can be a two-way experience between mentor and mentee. As teachers begin to share ideas with one another through the mentoring program, networking becomes important to continuous professional development for the future.

CHALLENGES FOR MENTORS

The major challenge for mentors is time. Finding time to do peer coaching during the day can be very difficult. Using planning periods to meet can be difficult because both teachers need to have the same time available. Finding time after school can also be challenging because that time is often filled by other professional commitments. Ideally, the mentor and the mentee should have regularly scheduled release time during the school day to meet and discuss the many issues related to first-year teaching.

The match between a mentor and a beginning teacher is important. Both individuals should have compatible teaching philosophies and mutual interests. Ideally, gender, age, and grade level or teaching assignment should be matched. According to Gordon (1990), the most effective matches are made between mentors and mentees who are the same gender, teach the same grade or subject matter, and have an age difference of eight to fifteen years.

Even though the intrinsic satisfaction of being a mentor is important and rewarding in and of itself, mentors should also be rewarded for their increased responsibilities with some tangible benefits. Compensation for their additional duties of mentoring might include additional salary in the form of a stipend, release time from teaching responsibilities, university tuition waivers, and travel funding for professional conferences (O'Dell, 1989). If a mentoring program is to be deemed valuable and important, then resources should be directed toward it to support the program and to provide compensation for those who make it work.

RESPONSIBILITIES OF THE MENTEE

A mentoring program is designed to help beginning teachers be successful, and the success of the mentoring program depends to a large degree on the mentee. To be mentored, one must accept assistance willingly and faithfully and must be committed to the mentoring process. Mentees must have trust and confidence in their mentor and be willing to discuss issues openly and truthfully with a sincere desire to learn. It is important for beginning teachers to recognize professional improvements and progress through frequent, systematic practice of reflection. Mentees should include their mentors in this reflection process. For the mentoring process to be successful, mentees need to be active in their own development and view learning as a continuous process. It is interesting to note that successful mentoring occurs when both the mentor and mentee recognize the mentoring relationship is reaching its natural end. In most cases, the mentoring relationship lasts for the academic school year.

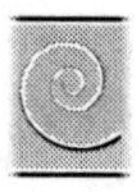

OUTCOMES OF THE MENTORING PROCESS

The expected outcome of the mentoring process is success for mentees in their teaching position. Ultimately, if the teacher receiving mentoring remains in the classroom and continues to teach effectively over a period of five years, then the mentoring process is ruled a true success. Another important outcome of a mentoring program is for the mentee to place high value on their mentoring experience and believe in the importance of a mentoring program. A truly successful outcome of the mentoring process is for mentees to go on to become mentors and use their former mentor as their role model.

SUMMARY

When highly effective teachers are asked which factors contributed to their success in the classroom, many point out the importance of their mentors during their first year of teaching. A mentor provides to the mentee moral support, guidance, and feedback as the mentee learns how to navigate successfully in the classroom. In addition, a mentor can help the mentee learn how to deal with professional issues through an analytical approach to solving problems. The essence of a mentoring program provides new teachers with supportive colleagues who are willing to share their experiences and expertise in helping new teachers become veteran teachers who are in turn successful in the classroom.

CASE STUDY

Casey Wade, a high school science teacher, is a beginning teacher and has been assigned a mentor, Mrs. Estrelle Arthur. Mrs. Arthur has taught chemistry for twenty-one years. She is viewed as one of the best science teachers in the county and she is passionate about her job. Her principal describes her as a dedicated professional who goes above and beyond expectations within the classroom and the school. From the beginning, Mrs. Arthur takes a real interest in Casey's success in the classroom. They have several conferences at the beginning of the year before the students arrive. Mrs. Arthur shares her many resources and asks Casey to write her professional goals as well as a personal discipline plan. Mrs. Arthur arranges for Casey to observe her teach several classes. Mrs. Arthur also schedules a monthly observation of Casey's class. Casey and Mrs. Arthur meet weekly to discuss various issues. In addition, Mrs. Arthur and Casey meet for dinner every couple of months. How would you rate this mentoring relationship? What are its strengths? What areas could be strengthened?

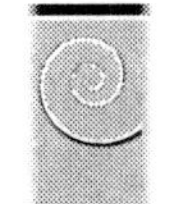

ACTIVITIES

1. Interview two individuals who have mentored a beginning teacher and interview two individuals who have recently been mentored. Identify successful and unsuccessful techniques used in the mentoring process.

2. Design an appropriate mentoring program for your school. If your school currently has a mentoring program, examine it, evaluate it, and make recommendations on how the program could be improved.

DISCUSSION QUESTIONS

1. Do you think mentors should be selected by the principal, colleagues, or through those who volunteer? Why? What are some other ways that mentoring programs can match mentors with mentees?

2. How much experience should mentors have before they begin mentoring? Why?

3. Is it possible to measure the success of a mentoring program? If so, how? If not, why?

REFERENCES

Bey, T. M. (1995, Nov). Mentorships. *Education & Urban Society, 28*(1), 11–20.

Gordon, S. P. (1990). *Assisting the Entry-Year Teacher. A Leadership Resource.* Columbus: Ohio Department of Education.

Halford, J. (1998). Easing the way for new teachers. *Educational Leadership, 55,* 33–36.

Henke, R. R., Chen, X., Geis, S., & Knepper, P. (2000). *Progress through the teacher pipeline: 1992–93 college graduates and elementary/secondary school teaching as of 1997.* NCES 2000–152. Washington, DC: National Center for Education Statistics.

Huling-Austin, L., & Murphy, S. C. (1987, April). *Assessing the impact of teacher induction programs: Implications for program development.* Paper presented at the Annual Meeting of the American Educational Research Association. Washington, D.C. (ERIC Document Reproduction Service No. ED 283 779).

Huling-Austin, L., O'Dell, S. J., Ishler, P., Kay, R. S., & Edelfelt, R. A. (1989). *Assisting the Beginning Teacher.* Reston, VA: Association for Teacher Educators.

Lohr, L. (1999, Spring). Assistance and review: Helping new teachers get started. *Teaching and Change, 6*(3), 295–314.

Moir, E. (1999). The stages of a teacher's first year. In M. Scherer (Ed.), *A Better Beginning: Supporting and Mentoring New Teachers* (pp. 241–251). London: Routledge Falmer.

O'Dell, S. A. (1990). *Mentor teacher programs.* Washington, D.C.: National Education Association.

Veenman, A. (1984). Perceived problems of beginning teachers. *Review of Educational Research, 54,* 143–178.

Villani, S. (1999). Mentoring new teachers: A good, strong anchor. In M. F. Hayes & I. K. Zimmerman (Eds.), *Teaching: A Career, a Profession* (pp. 19–25). Wellesley, MA: Massachusetts Association for Supervision and Curriculum Development.

Weinstein, C. S. (1988). Preservice teachers' expectations about the first year of teaching. *Teaching and Teacher Education, 4,* 31–40.

Chapter 9

Connecting with the Diverse Community

This chapter explores the importance of Teacher-Leader/Designers developing connections with students, families, and communities that are part of our diverse and multicultural society. This chapter will provide definitions, descriptions, and insights of the diverse populations found in today's society. In addition, readers will be provided with helpful suggestions on how to effectively teach and work with diverse and multicultural students, their families, and their communities.

After reading this chapter, you will be able to:

1. Explain why it is essential to connect with all students.
2. Describe why assessing the communities of students is important.
3. Identify different multicultural resources available in the community.
4. Explain why our classrooms are becoming more diverse.
5. Identify the major ethnic groups found in our classrooms.
6. Appraise future trends in the growth of diverse populations.
7. Identify the major religious beliefs found in our classrooms.
8. Identify the different languages spoken by students in our classrooms.
9. Explain the implications of PL 94–142 in our classrooms.
10. Describe appropriate teaching strategies for diverse classrooms.

WHY IS CONNECTING WITH STUDENTS, FAMILIES, AND THE COMMUNITY IMPORTANT?

Families and communities are vital to students' success and well-being within the school environment. When teachers address family involvement, they often cite the few parents, if any, who are involved within the school, often through parent-teacher conferences, as classroom volunteers, or through an organized Parent-Teacher Association. As the students get older, parental involvement often decreases. When trying to connect the classroom with the community, in many cases, teachers are unable to identify any real community involvement within their classrooms (Tellez, 2002). This lack of participation by families and communities makes successful education outcomes difficult. The belief that "It takes a village to raise a child' is true, and it should be an underlying belief in a Teacher-Leader/Designers' teaching philosophy (Clinton, 1996).

Teachers need to do more to involve families and the community in what takes place in their classrooms (Murrell & Diez, 1997). It is important that schools extend their roles far beyond traditional modes of involvement or, more accurately, lack of involvement. It is often left to Teacher-Leader/Designers to create opportunities for families and communities to connect within the schools and classrooms in meaningful ways and relationships.

Teacher-Leader/Designers need to design avenues that will include all parents as essential participants in the daily life of the classroom and as the most crucial supporters of their children's education at home. Connecting with the families of students informs teachers of the daily occurrences in the life of their students in areas such as hobbies and interests or significant events (Ziechner & Hoeft, 1996). In addition, when a working relationship is developed between teacher and parents, it allows teachers to communicate students' daily school experiences, strengths, and academic challenges. The students are able to see their teachers and parents as working partners who are helping them be successful both at school and at home.

Along with appropriate parental involvement, Teacher-Leader/Designers need to make sure their school is closely connected with the community. Schools and students are part of greater communities (Goodwin, 2002). In virtually all cases, there is a wealth of resources within the community that can enhance the educational experiences of all students (Wade, et al., 1999). Community members in all walks of life possess many talents and abilities that can be utilized as resources for learning in the classroom. In addition to connecting with individuals, involving the community also includes connecting with institutional agencies and organizations, such as the department of health, the department of social services, universities, museums, boys' and girls' clubs, Boy Scouts, Girl Scouts, the YMCA, and the local police department. When healthy relationships are formed between the classroom and community, students are provided with opportunities to understand how they are supported by a world that extends beyond their daily home and classroom environments (Gonzalez & Moll, 2002). In addition, students are able to observe their teachers working collaboratively with others outside the school.

The first step in creating and fostering a relationship among teachers, parents, and community is to know and understand the parents and community members (National Council for the Accreditation of Teacher Education, 2001). Teachers must not let their lack of knowledge or insecurities prevent them from learning and connecting with the families of their students (Rubio & Attinasi, 2000). However, connecting with parents and the community may be daunting and challenging for some teachers owing to the different demographics of these groups.

In many cases, a disparity exists between the demographics of the student populations in schools and that of the teaching profession. Approximately 88 to 90 percent of public school teachers are European-American and middle class, with the majority being female (National Center for Education Statistics, 2002). This homogeneous group of teachers often contrasts sharply with the multicultural populations of school children. If the current trends continue, the discrepancy between the two demographics will continue to increase in the coming years (Lewis, et al., 1999; Menken & Antunez, 2001). Teacher-Leader/Designers need to be proactive in learning about the different cultures of students in their classrooms and discover how to best meet the needs of this multicultural population.

SOCIETY CONTINUES TO BECOME MORE DIVERSE

Current classroom populations are quite different than those of the previous generation. High levels of immigration and mobility have made the multicultural classroom the norm rather than the exception. Almost 120 ethnic groups are represented in the United States. Mexican, Russian, Chinese, Indian, Philippine, Vietnamese, and Cuban ethnic groups account for more than 55 percent of the total non-white population.

Today, teachers are expected to teach effectively in all classrooms, including multicultural classrooms. However, many who teachers find themselves in such classrooms realize that their teacher education program did not adequately prepare them for this diversity (Tom, 1999). Teachers often find it challenging, and even threatening, to teach in multicultural classrooms. In many cases, the teachers are uncertain as to how they will be able to meet the needs of students from the various ethno-cultural and linguistic groups (Grant & Secanda, 1990). If they have no one to turn to in dealing with this increasingly common phenomenon, teachers can become frustrated, overwhelmed, and often choose to leave the profession because of their low teaching efficacy in teaching such diverse populations (Osborne, 1996). In these situations, Teacher-Leader/Designers are needed to step forward and assist their colleagues in adjusting to this new professional demand.

WHY HAVE OUR CLASSROOMS BECOME MORE MULTICULTURAL?

Two factors are primarily responsible for the increase of multicultural populations in our classrooms. The first factor is the immigration of populations from such diverse regions as the Middle East, Central and Latin

America, Southeast Asia and the Pacific, Eastern Europe, and Russia. Most of these populations look physically different from the mainstream population, which readily identifies them as being different. The second factor is the considerably higher birth rate among non-white populations than among whites. In the mid-1980s, approximately one in four children was a minority. By 2020, it is likely that this figure will increase to one child in two, and many of these children will be at the poverty level (Cushner, McClelland, & Safford, 2000). By 2050, the average U.S. resident, as defined by U.S. Census statistics, will be of African, Asian, Latin American, South Asian, or Middle Eastern heritage rather than European (National Center for Education Statistics, 1999).

DIFFERENT ETHNIC GROUPS FOUND IN THE SCHOOLS

Currently, many different cultures are found in our schools. It is important for educators to have some basic knowledge about each cultural group in order to better understand each unique culture. Some of the major cultural groups identified with some overview information related to each, follows.

African-Americans comprise 12.7% (35 million) of the total U.S. population. This population segment is expected to grow at nearly twice the rate of the rest of the population during the next fifty years (National Center for Educational Statistics, 2003). Seventy percent of African-American children are born into a single parent home and are likely to be living below the poverty level (An, Haven, & Wolfe, 1993; U.S. Department of Health and Human Services, 2001).

Arab-Americans are a growing population in America and can trace their roots to 22 countries in Africa and Asia and share a common language and heritage. While 66% of Arab-Americans are Christian, Muslims are the fastest growing segment (24%) of this community (Zooby, 2002). This group is more educated, more affluent, and more likely to own a business than the average American. The majority of Arab-Americans are born in America, and 82 percent are U.S. citizens and speak English fluently. The 2000 census estimates that four million Arab-Americans live in the United States.

Latinos comprise the fastest growing population in the country, with a 53-percent increase in the last ten years (U.S. Census, 2001). Mexican-Americans constitute the largest segment (86%) of the Latino group. Their growth rate is five times that of non-Latinos. In the year 2005, Latinos will constitute 13 percent (more than 36 million) of the population, making them the largest minority group in America. As this population grows, many Latinos are only partially assimilated into the English language and culture. Many prefer their own language and want to maintain their culture. Many Latinos maintain strong family units and live within the poverty level (Hispanic Dropout Project, 1998).

The Russian-American population, estimated at approximately three million people, a large, rapidly growing, and well-educated segment of the U.S. population. The Russian-born population represents the second largest segment of the U.S. population, accounting for 10.4 percent of the 28.4 million foreign-born Americans. The Russian-American population has a substantially higher per capita income and a higher level of wealth than the average American.

The largest Asian-American group is the Chinese, with a population of 2.5 million accounting for one quarter of the Asian-American population. Half of the Chinese-American population was born in China. This demographic group's average income is 30 percent higher than the national average, and the majority of this population own their homes. Chinese-Americans often seek quality and are value conscious with their economic resources. Chinese-American children are on average academically successful in their education.

Filipinos and Vietnamese populations also account for significant segments of the Asian-American population, comprising approximately 30 percent of that group (U.S. Dept. of Health and Human Services, 2001). Of the two, Filipinos tend to be better educated, more affluent, and more integrated into mainstream society. The majority of Vietnamese in the United States were born in Vietnam and still maintain many cultural influences in their homes. Both groups are viewed as hard-working, law-abiding citizens.

The two million Indian-Americans living in the United States are the third largest Asian-American population. About 50 percent of this population was born in India, 25 percent in the United States, and 25 percent in other countries. This population is the fastest growing Asian community group in the country, with a growth rate of 105.9 percent from 1990 to 2000 (U.S. Census, 2000). The Indian-American population has the highest annual income of any U.S. immigrant group. Over 90 percent of Indian-Americans speak English and at least one other language, and they live in nuclear families.

RELIGIOUS PLURALISM OF STUDENTS IN AMERICA

The United States was founded on religious freedom. The founding fathers clearly stated in the Constitution that religion and state must be kept separate. For this reason, Teacher-Leader/Designers must always make sure that they never advocate any religious beliefs in the classroom and always respect the religious beliefs of their students. However, this religious pluralism in our society has many educational implications in terms of curriculum materials, subject matter, school rules, school calendar decisions, cafeteria offerings, holiday celebrations, and teaching methods (Cushner, McClelland, & Safford, 2000).

The major religions found in U.S. society are Christianity, Judaism, Muslim, Hinduism, and Buddhism. Within each of these major religions are particular denominations (e.g., Christian denominations include Protestants, Catholics, Seventh-Day Adventists, and others). There are Orthodox, Conservative, and Moderate Jews. In the Muslim faith there are the Nation of Islam, Sunni, and Shiite groups. The same is true of Hinduism and Buddhism also contain different groups. The common thread among all of these religious groups is that they have clearly defined beliefs and customs that are an integral part of their culture (Bennett, 1999). The more Teacher-Leader/Designers learn about all religious groups, the more they will be able to respect and understand the diversity of the student populations found in our classrooms.

LANGUAGES FOUND IN THE SCHOOLS

In addition to the ethnic and religious diversity found in our schools, linguistic diversity also exists. More and more students are entering our classrooms with language skills in languages other than English. These children often have little or no competence in the English language. Spanish is the predominant foreign language of students entering our classrooms. In fact, the United States currently is the fifth largest Spanish-speaking country in the world (Becket, 1998). However, an increasing number of students are entering the schools speaking Arabic, Somali, Chinese, Hmong, Thai, Vietnamese, and Russian. It is not uncommon to find classrooms across America in which multiple languages other than English are the primary means of verbal communication of the students.

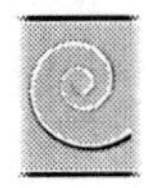

DIFFERENCES IN STUDENT ABILITIES

A significant change has impacted our classrooms since the enactment of The Education of All Handicapped Children Act of 1975 (PL 94–142). This federal law ensures that all children, regardless of any disability, are to be provided with a public school education. In 1990, this law was amended and renamed The Individuals with Disabilities Education Act, with the major change being that public education and assistance were provided for individuals up to age 21. Inclusion is the current trend for students with disabilities, which means that such students are spending more time in the traditional classroom learning along with their nondisabled peers. Teacher-Leader/Designers embrace this opportunity to include all children in their classrooms. They realize that nondisabled children can learn much from their peers with physical disabilities or other limitations.

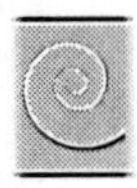

MAKING EDUCATION WORK IN THE DIVERSE CLASSROOM

The first step in being effective Teacher-Leader/Designers in classrooms containing children of diverse backgrounds is to acknowledge that all students have certain commonalities and needs, such as acceptance, belonging, achievement, and success. The second step is that Teacher-Leader/Designers need to fully believe that given adequate support, all children *can* learn, regardless of ethnic or cultural background, language, religious belief, and physical characteristics. The third step is to value the richness that diversity brings into the classroom and view it as an opportunity to enhance the learning experiences of all students. The following are some suggestions to deal effectively and proactively with children of diverse backgrounds.

Teachers should personalize learning for each student. Involve students and parents in making decisions that involve student learning. Always communicate in positive terms with students and parents, and make sure that you actively listen to them. It is important that Teacher-Leader/Designers learn as much as they can about their students and their culture; this is best accomplished through listening. A variety of teaching strategies always serve the students well. Students possess different learning styles and enjoy varied instruction. It is also important to use teaching strategies that emphasize collaborative and cooperative learning while deemphasizing competitive learning. Finally, establish and maintain high expectations for all students, not necessarily the same expectations for each student. Most important, communicate a sense of mutual respect to all students.

CONNECTING WITH THE COMMUNITY

The development of relationships with members of the community will occur only if Teacher-Leader/Designers make it happen. This important connection between the classroom and the community usually begins with Teacher-Leader/Designers surveying resources found within the local community, including businesses and organizations in operation, and identifying community leaders. Once this information has been collected and assessed, Teacher-Leader/Designers can connect these resources with specific units and lessons of instruction, as well as the specific learning needs of their students. This connection is usually accomplished simply by asking the appropriate individuals or organizations to be involved (Alexander, Heaviside, & Farris, 1999). In most cases, the individuals and organizations will be flattered and will graciously extend their assistance.

SUMMARY

Teacher-Leader/Designers must view twenty-first century classrooms, with all of their diversity and changes, as opportunities and resources rather than problems and deficits. It is important that Teacher-Leader/Designers help other teachers learn to feel comfortable and operate effectively within the dynamic environment of diverse classrooms and schools. Teacher-Leader/Designers will need to acquire an understanding of differences and interpersonal skills beyond the traditional pedagogy they were taught. Teacher-Leader/Designers must internalize these skills, perspectives, and attitudes in order to help the classrooms and schools connect through the students, families, and communities they serve.

CASE STUDY

Sally Pate was excited but nervous about her first day with her third-grade students. This was Sally's first teaching job and she wasn't sure she had made a good choice to teach at Lincoln Heights Elementary School. Police cars constantly patrolled the school's neighborhood. On each side of the street leading to the school were garbage-strewn, dilapidated apartment buildings. The neighborhood contained many abandoned buildings occupied by drug dealers, addicts, and the homeless. As the children excitedly entered her classroom on that first day, Sally was quick to assess that her class was the epitome of a multicultural diversity. At least five nationalities and four languages besides English were represented in her class of 24 students. This class definitely was not like her university practicums and internships, nor was it like anything she had experienced growing up. Sally had been exposed only to white, middle-class people in all aspects of her everyday life. At the end of the day, Sally went home in tears and called her mother, a veteran teacher of 22 years. As Sally explained to her mother, she could never teach children who had to always worry about their next meal, hot water, clothes, and shelter. She stated that her students probably couldn't even get a decent night's sleep because of all the gunfire heard in the neighborhood. When Sally's mother, a Teacher-Leader/Designer, finally had a chance to speak to Sally during their conversation, she stated that these children had the same basic needs of all children, and as soon as Sally identified each of her students as individuals, she could start to make a difference in their lives. What other advice could Sally's mother give her? What are some appropriate teaching strategies that might help Sally be effective in her classroom?

ACTIVITIES

1. Locate and interview an individual who emigrated to the United States in the last ten years. Ask questions such as what did this person expect people and life to be like in the United States? To what extent have the initial expectations been confirmed? What does this individual like best about the United States? What is most difficult?

2. Imagine that you have been selected to speak, on behalf of all teachers in your state, to your state legislators regarding funding issues for education. Your topic is multicultural education. Choose the topic "The Case Against Multicultural Education" or "The Case for Multicultural Education" and write a three-page speech that you would deliver to the legislators.

DISCUSSION QUESTIONS

1. Why does Black History Month sometimes trigger resentment among non–African-American students? How might the goals and objectives of Black History Month be best achieved in your classroom?

2. What are the arguments for and against school programs that include Christian beliefs, music, and traditions, such as Christmas or Easter programs? How should a Teacher-Leader/Designer handle the controversy?

3. As a Teacher-Leader/Designer, you want to lead the way in including a comprehensive multicultural education in your classroom. What are the five most difficult problems that you anticipate? How would you overcome these problems?

REFERENCES

Alexander, D., Heaviside, S., & Farris, E. (1999). *Status of Educational Reform in Public Elementary and Secondary Schools: Teachers' Perspectives.* Washington, D.C.: U.S. Dept. of Education, National Center for Education Statistics.

An, C., Haven, R., & Wolfe, B. (1993). Teen out-of-wedlock births and welfare receipt: The role of childhood events and economic circumstances. *Review of Economics and Statistics, 75*(2), 195–208.

Becket, D. R. (1998). Increasing the number of Latino and Navajo teachers in hard-to-staff schools. *Journal of Teacher Education, 49*(3), 196–206.

Bennett, C. I. (1999). *Comprehensive Multicultural Education: Theory and Practice* (4th ed.). Boston: Allyn and Bacon.

Clinton, H. R. (1996). *It Takes a Village.* New York: Simon & Schuster.

Cushner, K., McClelland, A., & Safford. (2000). *Human Diversity in Education: An Integrative Approach* (3rd ed.). New York: McGraw-Hill.

Gonzalez, N., & Moll, L. (2002). Cruzando el Puente: Building bridges to funds of knowledge. *Educational Policy, 16*(4), 623–641.

Goodwin, A. L. (2002). Teacher preparation and the education of immigrant children. *Education and Urban Society, 34*(2), 156–172.

Grant, C. A. & Secanda, W. G. (1990). Preparing teachers for diversity. In R. Houston (Ed.), *Handbook of Research on Teacher Education* (pp. 403–422). New York: Macmillan.

Hispanic Dropout Project. (1998). Final report. Available online at http://www.ncela.gwu.edu/miscpubs/hdp/final.htm.

Lewis, L., Parsad, B., Carey, N., Bartfai, N., Farris, E., & Smerdon, B. (1999). *Teacher quality: A report on the preparation and qualifications of public school teachers.* Washington, D.C.: U.S. Dept. of Education, Office of Educational Research and Improvement, National Center for Education Statistics.

Menken, K., & Antunez, B. (2001). *An Overview of the Preparation and Certification of Teachers Working with Limited English Proficient (LEP) Students.* Washington, D.C.: National Clearinghouse for Bilingual Education.

Murrell, P. Jr., & Diez, M. E. (1997). A model program for educating teachers for diversity. In J. E. King, E. R. Hollins, & W. C. Hayman (Eds.), *Preparing teachers for cultural diversity* (pp. 113–128). New York: Teachers College Press.

National Center for Educational Statistics. (1999). *National Assessment of Educational Progress, 1999 Long-term Assessment.* Washington, D.C.: NCES.

National Center for Educational Statistics. (2002). *Common Core of Data Survey.* Washington, D.C.: NCES.

National Center for Educational Statistics. (2003). *The Condition of Education 2003.* Washington, D.C.: NCES.

National Council for the Accreditation of Teacher Education. (2001). *Professional Standards for the Accreditation of Schools, Colleges, and Departments of Education.* Washington, D.C.: NCATE.

Osborne, A. B. (1996). Practice into theory into practice: Culturally relevant pedagogy for students we have marginalized and normalized. *Anthropology and Education Quarterly, 27*(3), 285–314.

Rubio, O. G., & Attinasi, J. (2000). Teachers in post-proposition-227 Southern California: Implications for teacher education. *Journal of Instructional Psychology, 27*(4), 273–287.

Tellez, K. (2002). Multicultural education as subtext. *Multicultural Perspectives, 4*(2), 21–26.

Tom, A. R. (1997). *Redesigning Teacher Education.* Albany, NY: State University of New York Press.

U.S. Census. (2001). *A Report of Demographic Movements.* Washington, D.C.: U.S. Census Bureau.

U.S. Dept. of Health and Human Services. (2001). *Trends in the Well-Being of America's Children and Youth, 2000.* Washington, D.C.: Author.

Wade, R. C., Anderson, J. B., Yarborough, D. B., Pickeral, T., Erickson, J. A., & Kromer, T. (1999). Novice teachers' experiences of community service-learning. *Teaching and Teacher Education, 15,* 667–684.

Ziechner, K. M., & Hoeft, K. (1996). Teacher socialization for cultural diversity. In J. Sikula (Ed.), *Handbook of Research in Teacher Education* (2nd ed.), (pp. 525–547), New York: Macmillian.

Zooby, J. (2002). *Arab-Americans in United States According to the U.S. Census.* Accessed online March 6, 2005, at http://www.johnzooby.org.

Chapter 10

Collaborating with Teachers, Administrators, and the Community

This chapter will explore the importance of possessing effective collaboration skills for Teacher-Leader/Designers. It first describes underlying assumptions and benefits as well as the importance of collaborating with other teachers. This chapter also provides a definition of action learning and its associated principles. It discusses Peter Senge's concept of a learning organization and its corresponding five disciplines. This chapter then lists specific qualities of effective learning communities and examples of face-to-face and online learning communities. This chapter concludes by discussing how collaboration, action learning principles, Senge's learning organization, and learning communities can be effective alternatives to traditional in-service teacher professional development.

After reading this chapter, you will be able to:

1. Define the underlying assumptions of collaborative learning.
2. Describe the benefits of collaborative learning.
3. Describe the importance of collaborative learning.
4. Describe action learning and its principles.
5. Describe Peter Senge's learning organization concept and its five disciplines.
6. Describe the qualities of a learning community.
7. List examples of face-to-face learning communities and online learning communities.
8. Describe the potential impact of collaborative learning on existing in-service professional development practices.

WHAT IS COLLABORATION?

When one considers the concept of collaboration, one can refer to several related terms. Collaborative learning (e.g., Barkley, Cross, & Major, 2005; Villalobos, Eshilian, & Moyer, 2005) refers to collaboration between students. LaPlant and Zane's (2005) *Partner Learning Systems* is an example of a collaborative learning program. Cooperative learning (e.g., Johnson & Johnson, 1994) also is quite similar to collaborative learning and refers to cooperative learning activities between students. Thousand, Villa, and Nevin's (2005) Cooperative Group Lesson plans are an example of cooperative learning. In this chapter, we focus exclusively on the collaboration between teachers, action learning (a form of collaborative learning), a learning organization, learning communities, and the impact of collaborative learning on in-service teacher professional development. Overall, we define collaborative learning between teachers as a team of two or more teachers striving to achieve shared learning goals, such as developing a third-grade science unit, organizing an in-service professional development seminar on classroom management, integrating streaming videos into an existing unit on frog dissection, or other similar activities. The key element of collaboration is that teachers work together and support each other in performing one or more of their professional duties. Understanding the role of collaboration and associated activities will strengthen the skills of Teacher-Leader/Designers and will add to their expertise.

WHAT ARE ASSUMPTIONS AND BENEFITS OF COLLABORATION?

We are definitive advocates of collaboration among teachers. Our unreserved endorsement is based on undeniable assumptions about teachers and the role of a Teacher-Leader/Designer. First of all, teaching does *not* occur in a vacuum. That is, teachers constantly work with their colleagues, assistant principals, principal, school district curriculum directors, and possibly students in designing quality lessons. Although it may seem as though a teacher works in isolation in the classroom and is recognized as the leader in this particular setting, it is increasingly important, and indeed required, for teachers to work and collaborate with others. This situation is constructive and brings to mind a familiar adage, "Two heads are better than one." Teaching and student learning is enhanced when more than one "head" or teacher work together. We concur with Barkley, Cross, & Major's (2005) assertion, "Meaningful and lasting learning occurs through personal, active engagement." Changing the role of the isolated teacher to that of collaborative teacher will transform the role of a school and ultimately increase student learning.

There are several benefits of active teacher collaboration. By collaborating, one is exposed to a variety of perspectives. These perspectives and new ideas definitely enrich one's professional development and create an atmosphere of lifelong learning (Mills, 2000). Barkley, Cross, and Major (2005) declared that some of the qualities of effective teacher collaboration include positive interdependence, as well as individual and group accountability. Most important, we believe that a key benefit of effective teacher collaboration is that it engages teachers in the reflective process and elevates the importance of active learning among colleagues.

WHY IS EFFECTIVE COLLABORATION IMPORTANT?

Effective collaboration among colleagues in any professional setting is becoming increasingly essential and necessary for a productive teamwork environment. As our society transitions from the Information Age to the Knowledge Age, an effective collaborative workforce is an expectation for the twenty-first century. This is particularly true for teachers and Teacher-Leader/Designers. In his book on teaching in the Knowledge Age, Hargreaves (2003) wrote, "Teachers, more than anyone, are expected to build learning communities, create the knowledge society and develop the capacities for innovation, flexibility, and commitment to change that are essential to economic prosperity." If teachers and Teacher-Leader/Designers are expected to be the catalysts for ensuring a healthy transition to Knowledge Age, we advocate that teachers must have effective collaborative skills within both the classroom and their respective schools. Teachers must demonstrate effective strategies for working together to create knowledge. The benefit of this knowledge creation will demonstrate the effectiveness of individuals working together and how this process enriches the entire collaborative experience.

ACTION LEARNING AND ITS RELATIONSHIP WITH COLLABORATION

One of the formalized ways to promote and initiate collaborative practices among individuals, including teachers, is to adopt action learning practices and principles. Action learning was established as a way to reform individual organizations, encourage individuals to analyze specific problems within an organization, propose solutions to these problems and, most important, provide action learning participants the opportunity to consciously develop their own learning. Patton (2002) describes action learning as "inquiry within organizations aimed at learning, improvement and development." The action learning is intended to "help a group of people reflect on ways of improving what they are doing or understand it in new ways" (Patton, 2002). Similar to the purpose of action research (see chapter 7), the focus of action learning is on continuous improvement. Organizations such as schools should have "an unwavering commitment to progress" (Zmuda, Kuklis, & Kline, 2004). Teachers can join "reflective action learning groups" in which colleagues share their findings and interpretations and, most important, participate in a lifelong learning process. Patton (2002, p. 180) notes that there are two outcomes from the action learning process: "the inquiry can yield specific insights and findings that can change practice"; and "those who participate in the inquiry learn to think more systemically about what they are doing and their own relationship to those with whom they work." Again, similar to action research, action learning participants need to be willing to take risks and "action," as well as be willing developers of a functioning action learning community.

PETER SENGE'S LEARNING ORGANIZATION

To realize the potential of action learning principles and to implement such principles, Peter Senge (1990) proposed and defined the concept of a learning organization. Action learning and reflective practice are the building blocks of a learning organization (Patton, 2002). According to Smith (2001), Senge's learning organizations enable individuals to

> continually expand their capacity to create the results they truly desire, where new and expansive patterns of thinking are nurtured, where collective aspiration is set free, and where people are continually learning to see the whole together.

Individuals who work in a learning organization want to continually improve their professional skills and to collaborate with their colleagues in meeting this common lifelong learning goal. One of the premises of Senge's learning organization is that successful organizations need to be flexible, adaptive, and productive (Smith, 2001). Learning organizations should enable members to continually learn and have the capacity to create new experiences. Senge and associates (O'Neil, 1995; Senge, et al., 2000) have extensively explored ways in which a school can become a learning organization, or a "school that learns."

According to Senge, there are five aspects or disciplines that are at the core of a learning organization. Learning organization members must master and continually practice these disciplines in order to create an active and innovative learning organization. These five disciplines are described below.

- *Personal mastery* A learning organization encourages and requires its participants to be in continual learning mode (Smith, 2001). The intent of this learning is to strive toward mastering personal and professional goals. It is the "practice of articulating a coherent image of your personal vision—the results you most want to create in your life . . ." (Senge, et al., 2000).
- *Shared vision* Not only does a learning organization promote lifelong learning, it institutes an environment that encourages participants to build and vocalize a common vision. The goal is to "hold a shared picture of the future we seek to create" (Senge, 1990). Individuals build this shared vision by determining a common purpose through a continuing dialogue with each other. Senge reminds us, "A school or community that hopes to live by learning needs a common shared vision process" (Senge, et al., 2000).
- *Mental models* The key to constructing a shared vision is to decipher and comprehend individuals' mental models. Originally described by Kenneth Craik in 1943, "mental models are representations in the mind of real or imaginary situations" (Johnson-Laird & Byrne, 2000).

Everyone has a mental model that corresponds to a particular concept or situation. For example, an eighth-grade teacher will have a mental model of her particular school. Both her principal and students also will have a mental model of the same school. However, each mental model will differ and will correspond to each individual's perception of the particular school. Senge (1990) asserts that mental models are "deeply ingrained assumptions, generalizations, or even pictures and images that influence how we understand the world and how we take action." Members of a learning organization must be cognizant of their own mental models and how these models interact with those of their colleagues. Learning organizations need to promote an openness where individuals' thinking is exposed.

- *Team learning* Senge labeled team learning as the "discipline of group interaction" (Senge, et al., 2000) and as "the process of aligning and developing the capacities of a team to create the results its members truly desire" (Senge, 1990). This collaboration among teachers actually is composed of both the personal mastery and shared vision disciplines. To foster team learning, Senge describes and advocates discussion techniques that encourage learning organization members to be in continuous dialogue.
- *Systems thinking* In order to create a learning organization, individuals should "learn to better understand interdependency and change" (Senge, et al., 2000) or develop systems thinking. Individuals must see and understand the intricacies of how their action affects others within the entire system. To further understand this perspective, Senge illustrates the systems affecting a school through three nested systems (see Figure 10.1). In a school setting, teachers, students, and parents are three main groups that affect an individual school. However, there are other influential factors, such as a superintendent, administrative and support staff, the school board and other stakeholders. Furthermore, additional factors, such as community institutions, local media, and a local university, can also impact the activities of a school. By adopting a *Systems Thinking* perspective, one sees all of the influencing factors within a particular system and becomes aware of how each relationship can affect a school by a single action.

To be able to transform and lead a learning organization, a new view of leadership is required. Peter Senge argues that the "traditional view of leaders, as special people who set the direction, make key decisions and energize the troops as deriving from a deeply individualistic and non-systemic worldview" (Smith, 2001) "is based on assumptions of people's powerlessness, their lack of personal vision and inability to master the forces of change, deficits which can be remedied only by a few great leaders" (Senge, 1990). Senge's learning organization, action learning principles, and learning communities for professional development contradict these assumptions. By proposing a learning organization, one essentially is questioning whether an organization has a learning disability. To transition from a traditional organizational mindset to a learning organization mindset, there is a definitive need for shared leadership and defining a shared vision (Roberts & Pruitt, 2003).

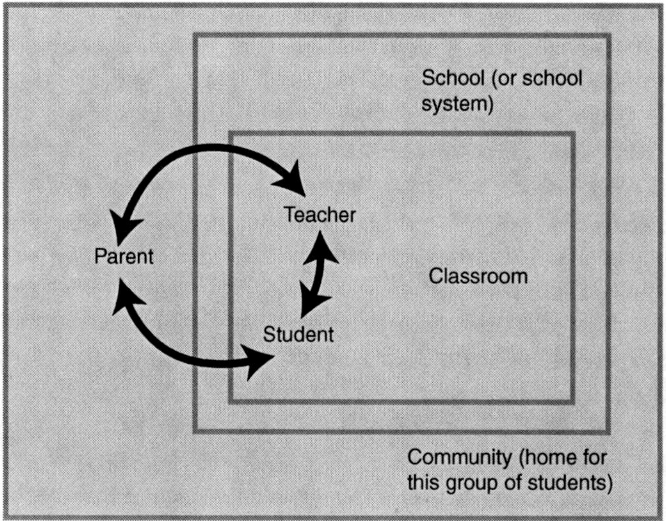

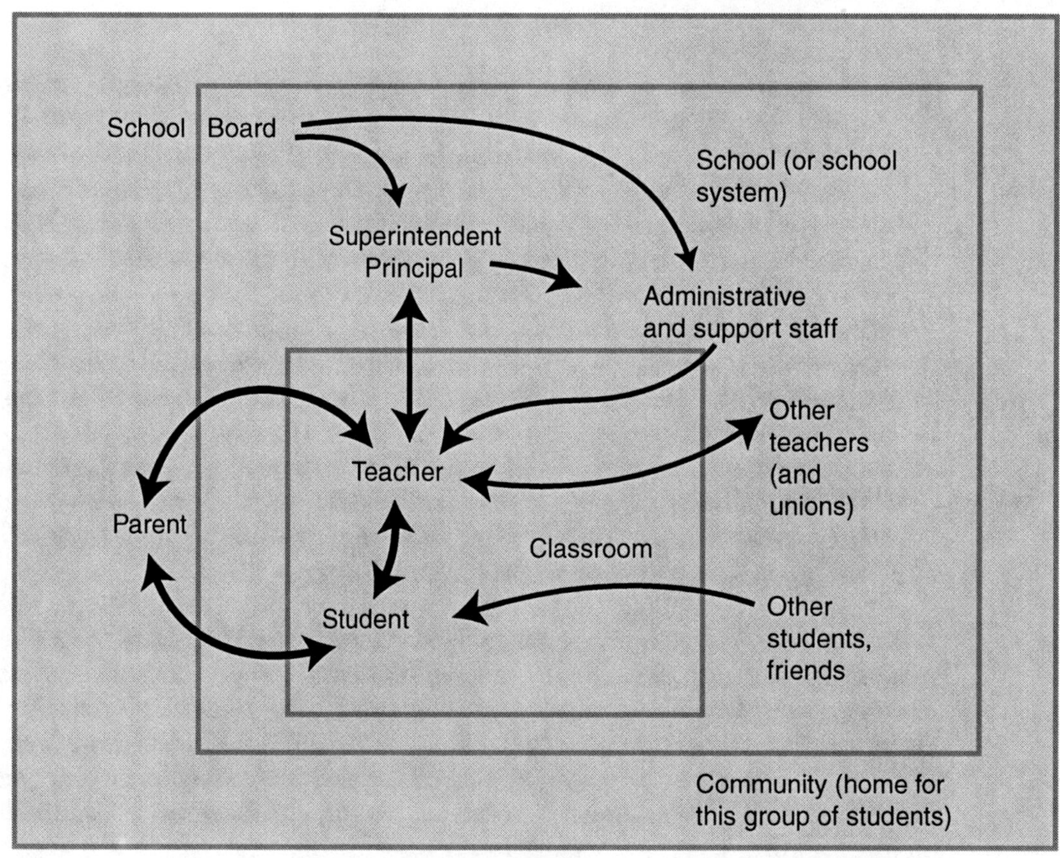

Figure 10.1 Three nested systems affecting public schools. (Senge, 2000, et al.)

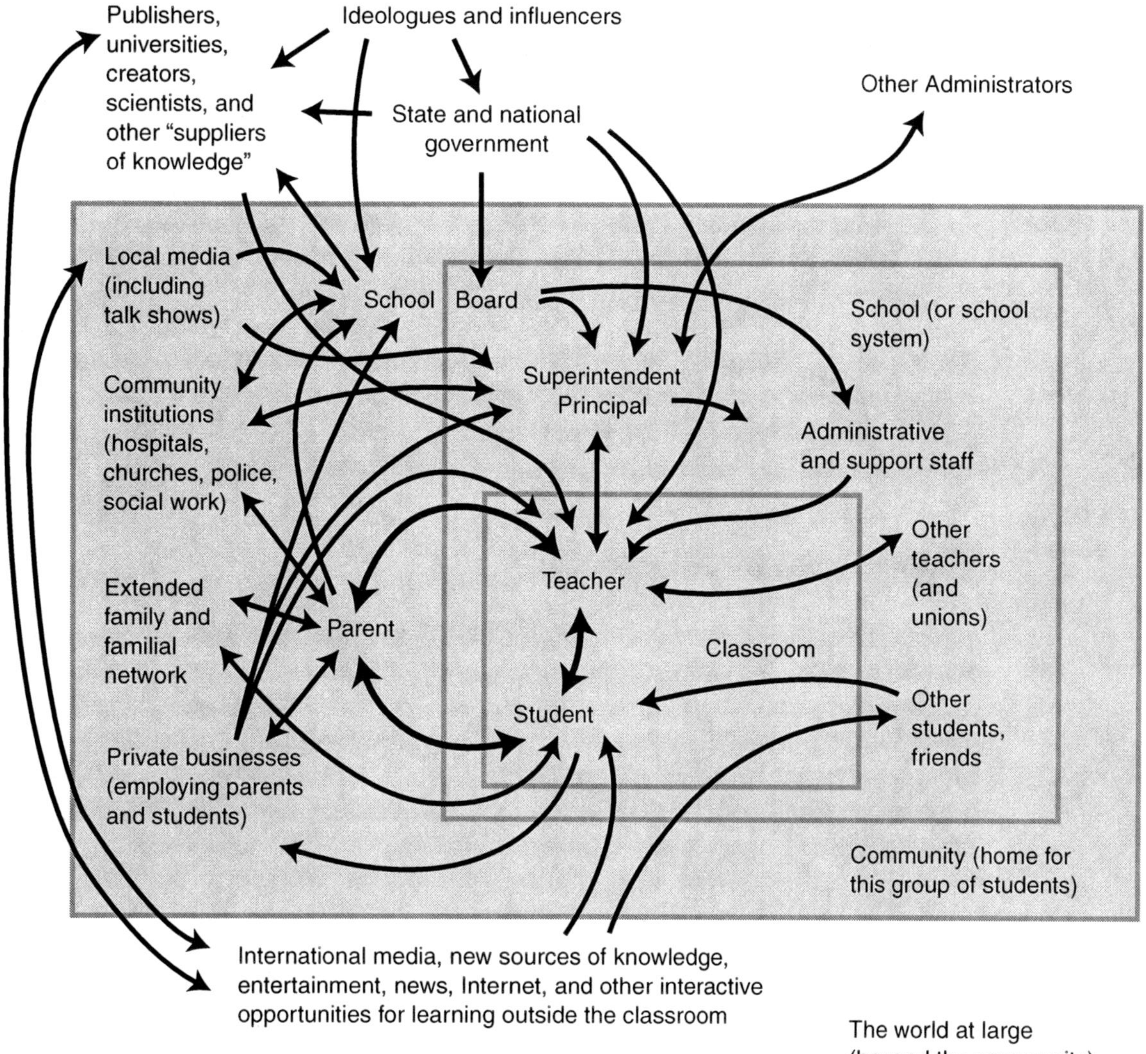

Figure 10-1

This acknowledged perspective shift creates three new roles for a leader: *Leader as Designer, Leader as Steward,* and *Leader as Teacher.* A *Leader as Designer* concept is quite similar to a Teacher-Designer and a Teacher-Leader/Designer. Smith (2001) observed, "The functions of design are rarely visible . . . yet no one has a more sweeping influence than the designer." The main *Leader as Designer* responsibilities concentrate on developing effective organizational policies, which enable each of the five learning organization disciplines, such as building a shared vision. A *Leader as Steward* ability acknowledges the leader's role in "owning" the vision of a learning organization. Effective leaders must make a commitment to managing and leading their respective organizations. They also must realize that they do not own the vision, but simply are stewards that facilitate the process in developing this shared vision. A *Leader as Teacher* capability acknowledges the need for leaders to teach. This type of leader needs to "cultivate an understanding of what the organization (and its members) are seeking to become" (Smith, 2001). According to Smith (2001), a *Leader as Teacher* is

> . . . not about "teaching" people how to achieve their vision. It is about fostering learning, for everyone. Such leaders help people throughout the organization develop systemic understandings. Accepting this responsibility is the antidote to one of the most common downfalls of otherwise gifted teachers—losing their commitment to the truth.

An effective learning organization requires not only the integration of Senge's five disciplines, but it also demands a new type of leader. We expect Teacher-Leader/Designers to be actively involved in this proposed formation of the learning organization mindset within schools.

LEARNING COMMUNITIES

During the past fifteen years and since Peter Senge originally proposed the formation of a learning organization, several learning communities based on the Senge's five disciplines have developed. Roberts and Pruitt (2003) declared, "In recent years, the school reform literature has begun to reflect a view of schools as communities of learners." These authors also state, learning communities are an "effective model for fostering school improvement" and have "profound effects on the members of a school community." Roberts and Pruitt (2003) also observed five new teacher roles affected by a learning community: teachers as colleagues; teachers as leaders; teachers as learners; teacher-parent relationships; and teachers as pedagogues. Teachers as pedagogues share "teaching strategies, planning for instruction, and looking for new ways to learn" (Roberts & Pruitt, 2003). These skills are quite similar to a Teacher-Designer. These learning communities are definitively impacting the public schools by changing existing schools into communities of learners that include teachers, administrators, and students.

Definable characteristics of learning communities become apparent when utilizing and applying Senge's five disciplines. Kruse, Louis, and Bryk (1995) observed that reflective dialogue, collective focus on student learning, collaboration, and shared values and norms all are common qualities of effective learning communities. The School Change Collaborative (2005) proposes that supportive and shared leadership, collective creativity, shared values and vision, conditions that support a learning organization, and shared personal practice all are characteristics of a school learning community. Stinnette, Peterson, and Hallinger (2005) have developed a checklist that helps teachers to reflect on leadership and corresponding practices at their respective schools. This list of questions gives an indication on whether a school possesses the characteristics of a learning community. The *Directory of Consultants for Learning Communities* (Coalition for Self-Learning, 2001) lists the myriad of grassroots groups that are now involved with the development of learning communities. These resources offer a multitude of information regarding learning communities to help schools to consider how to become effective, dynamic learning communities.

EXISTING LEARNING COMMUNITIES

Currently, school learning communities are forming at an increasing rate. Each of these learning communities is based on the action learning discipline, Senge's learning organization disciplines, and collaborative learning principles. Examples of three learning communities are described below.

- *Coalition For Self-Learning* (2005): This organization essentially serves as a learning community clearinghouse and information resource. This coalition "envisions and co-creates a world of cooperative life-long learning communities" and "promotes ideas and actions for creating learning communities." It provides online tools to promote learning communities, such as its *Creating Learning Communities* website (http://www.CreatingLearningCommunities.org) and hosts two discussion groups. (See groups.yahoo.com/group/LearningCommunities, and groups.yahoo.com/community/CCL-LLCs.)
- *Ohio Department of Education* (2002): Ohio's *Transforming Learning Communities* studied twelve high-performing schools and how best to develop learning communities. It is noted, "school change is driven by the development of 'learning communities' within schools. But little is known about how these communities come together to enrich and transform the learning experience." This project attempted to answer the overall question, "How do learning communities develop and what can be done to strengthen and speed up their urgent reforms?" This project observed, "Learning communities do not develop in a 'perfect' world. School change is by its nature nonlinear, chaotic, 'messy.'" The group stressed the need for collaboration among teachers and student. It found, "'Successful teaming' is essential for school change, for teachers and students, at every level." The Ohio Department of Education plans to expand its twelve pilot programs and develop incentives that promote school learning communities. The project identified nine strategic actions. Some of these actions include: creating conditions that enable and stimulate innovation; developing cross-disciplinary learning experiences; expanding shared responsibility; and other similar initiatives.
- *School Change Collaborative* (2005): This project investigated the effectiveness of and need for school learning communities by employing a *Story Investigation Approach.* The premise of this approach is "every school has stories to tell." With the focus on learning communities, the goal is to "understand deeply a school's changes over time" and ask the following questions: "What does it really mean for a school to be a learning community? What does it look like? How does a school come to embody this approach? What external factors can assist the process?" During a two-day period, invited schools participated in a discussion involving the following topics: The purpose for the school's learning; the leadership that enabled and supported the journey; the

external influences that supported or provided expertise for the school's efforts; and the school's goals and how they are monitored and assessed; and information about their students. Responses to these questions gave insight on how best to structure and develop a learning community at these respective schools.

Each of these learning community programs and initiatives provide additional information and rationale for Teacher-Leader/Designers to start a learning community in their own schools.

ONLINE COLLABORATION AND LEARNING COMMUNITIES

In addition to the aforementioned learning communities, an online environment is an excellent setting for learning communities. Numerous online learning communities have been established during the past ten years. Some of these communities include: Bonk and colleagues' (2002) Teacher Institute for Curriculum Knowledge about the Integration of Technology (TICKIT); Leask and Younie's (2001) European Schoolnet; Topper and colleagues' (1997) LETSNet website; Bronack and colleagues' (1999) CaseNet; and Reynolds and colleagues' (2001) learning community, *The Internet Learning Forum.* These virtual environments provided an electronic apprenticeship for the teachers. That is, teachers were able to confer and collaborate with peers and experts concerning technology integration-related activities in an online environment. Harvard University's (2005) Education with New Technologies website is a learning community "designed to help educators develop powerful learning experiences for students through the effective integration of new technologies." It provides access to fellow teacher educators throughout the world by providing online tutorials, a collaborative curriculum design tool, online threaded discussions, and an online resource library. Georgia Institute of Technology (2005) provides an online resource that promotes and displays their research on the design of communities on the Internet. This research perspective is "inspired by an educational theory called constructionism—the idea that people learn best when they are making something that is personally meaningful to them." The groups is particularly interested in how "communities of learners can motivate and support one another's learning experiences." It believes that "computer networks have the potential to facilitate community-supported constructionist learning." We share the same belief. Teacher-Leader/Designers can reap many benefits from participating in asynchronous activities (e.g., threaded discussions) and synchronous activities (e.g., chats) with other teachers in an online learning community.

IMPACT ON INSERVICE TEACHER PROFESSIONAL DEVELOPMENT

There is no doubt that existing professional development programs need to be revised. Mouza (2002) noted, "Traditional sit-and-get training sessions without follow-up support have not been effective in preparing teachers to integrate classroom technologies. Rather thoughtful and ongoing professional development programs are needed" (p. 273). Conventional one-day, in-service technology workshops (usually conducted during after school or during a teacher inservice day) are inadequate. To be effective, future workshops must concentrate on the long-term development of teacher skills (Bonk, et al., 2002). We believe that collaborative learning, action learning, Senge's learning organization, and learning communities can provide alternatives to traditional inservice professional development activities and to promote lifelong learning. Collaborating with other teachers within an established learning community is an excellent way to provide ongoing support.

Roberts and Pruitt (2003) have proposed a variety of alternatives based on learning community principles, including: collaborative professional development; job-embedded professional development; and school-based professional development. In fact, the Coalition of Essential Schools (2005) offers a *Critical Friends Group* (or learning community) approach for inservice teachers' professional development needs: "A Critical Friends Group (CFG) brings together six to ten teachers within a school over at least two years, to help each other look seriously at their own classroom practice and make changes in it." By encouraging teachers to collaborate and participate in a learning community, the professional development workshop format will ultimately be replaced by a professional development learning community format.

THE VALUE OF POSSESSING COLLABORATION SKILLS

The ability to implement action learning principles and the five disciplines of Senge's learning organization depends on actively practicing collaboration skills. Continually collaborating with other teachers and administrators is the essential building block of a working learning community. Roberts and Pruitt (2003) concur: "Collaboration is the vital factor in the development and maintenance of professional learning communities. Without collaboration, there would be no learning communities." Teachers will face specific challenges in becoming effective collaborators. In order to overcome these obstacles, they must adopt a learning organization (and the corresponding five disciplines) mindset and work effectively with their colleagues. We are quite confident that teachers who adopt a Teacher-Leader/Designer perspective will readily become effective collaborators. This innovative outlook will ensure successful school learning communities that offer valuable student learning outcomes.

SUMMARY

Teacher-Leader/Designers need to increase their collaboration skills and activities with their colleagues. Such skills and activities are critical to providing a quality education and creating an effective school environment for twenty-first century schools. Understanding and applying action learning principles, Senge's learning organization's five disciplines, and the characteristics of effective learning communities will ensure this quality education and effective school environment. By becoming active collaborators with fellow teachers, administrators, parents, students, and other appropriate individuals, Teacher-Leader/Designers will make sure that this transition from an Information Age school to a Knowledge Age school will take place. More important, a collaborative teacher will achieve a successful livelihood as a Teacher-Leader/Designer.

CASE STUDY

After school principal Warren Zucker returned from a workshop entitled "What kind of school are you?: Implementing Peter Senge's five disciplines into the Green Vale school district," he told his secretary, Nora Samuels, to find a free one-hour block in his busy schedule. Zucker realized that he needed this time to review and begin to implement his workshop notes. He knew that the new superintendent, Dr. Eliza Dillon, would follow-up on this workshop and would inquire how the seventeen Green Vale principals were going to transform their schools into "learning schools." Even though Dr. Dillon had inferred that the fifth discipline school mindset is optional, Zucker and his fellow principals knew that one of Dr. Dillon's top priorities was to "ensure a school learning community for Green Vale neighborhood schools." Dr. Dillon's apparent obsession with this idea traces back to her relationship with Dr. Bill Louis, her mentor at a local university. Apparently, Dr. Louis collaborated and co-authored two articles with Peter Senge. It is no wonder that Dr. Louis and two of his graduate students developed this recent workshop. After two days, Zucker finally was able to readjust his schedule and could review his notes. His head started to spin a little. He tried to remember the definitions and implications of terms, such as personal mastery, mental models, shared vision, and systems thinking. He remembered only the intricate systems thinking illustrations that Dr. Louis showed in his PowerPoint presentations. He also recalled hearing about a couple of teacher teams that work with each other on developing lesson units. Can he justify these respective teams as a learning community? He also wondered what other current activities he could justify as being a learning organization. What advice would you give Warren Zucker? How can he start investigating whether his school is already implementing the five disciplines? What are the next steps to start becoming a learning organization?

ACTIVITIES

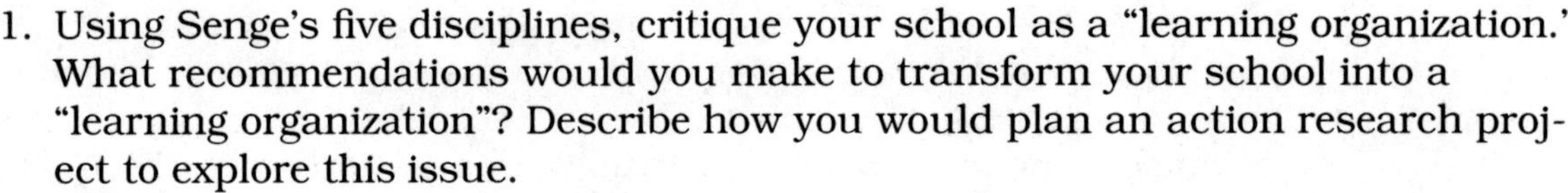

1. Using Senge's five disciplines, critique your school as a "learning organization." What recommendations would you make to transform your school into a "learning organization"? Describe how you would plan an action research project to explore this issue.

2. View and complete Stinnette, Peterson, and Hallinger's (2005) learning community checklist at: http://www.ncrel.org/cscd/pubs/lead21/2-1l.htm. Ask at least three teachers and the principal at your school to complete this checklist. Review all of the responses. Were there any disagreements about the respective responses? Discuss possible ways to improve your school as a learning community. Summarize your discussion and possible action items to implement a learning community at your school.

DISCUSSION QUESTIONS

1. Do you currently participate in existing informal or formal learning communities? If so, describe your experiences. If not, would you be interested in forming a learning community at your school? Why or why not?

2. Assess the current professional development offerings in your school district. How would you improve these offerings with respect to action learning, learning organization, and learning community principles?

3. We assert that the ability to collaborate with other teachers is critical to ensuring an effective school and positive student outcomes. Do you agree or disagree with this assertion? Explain your response, citing your previous experiences with collaboration.

REFERENCES

Barkley, K., Cross, P., & Major, C. H. (2005). *Collaborative Learning Techniques: A Handbook for College Faculty.* San Francisco: Jossey-Bass.

Bonk, C., Ehman, L., Hixon, E., & Yamagata-Lynch, L. (2002). Pedagogical TICKIT: Web conferencing to promote communication and support during teacher professional development. *Journal of Technology and Teacher Education, 10*(2), 205–233.

Bronack, S. C., Kilbane, C. R., Herbert, J. M., & McNergney, R. F. (1999). In-service and pre-service teachers' perceptions of a web-based, case-based learning environment. *Journal of Information Technology for Teacher Education, 8*(3), 305–320.

Coalition for Essential Learning. (2005). Critical friends groups. Retrieved April 28, 2005, from http://cesnorthwest.org/critical_friends_groups.htm.

Coalition for Self-Learning. (2001). Directory of consultants for creating learning communities. Retrieved May 6, 2005, from http://www.creatinglearningcommunities.org/resources/consultants.htm.

Coalition for Self-Learning. (2005). Creating learning communities' online resource center. Retrieved April 28, 2005, from http://www.creatinglearningcommunities.org/.

Georgia Institute of Technology. (2005). Electronic learning communities. Retrieved April 15, 2005, from http://www.cc.gatech.edu/elc/.

Hargreaves, A. (2003). *Teaching in the Knowledge Society: Education in the Age of Insecurity.* New York: Teachers College Press.

Harvard University. (2005). Education with new technologies: Networked learning community. Retrieved May 6, 2005, from http://learnweb.harvard.edu/ent/home/index.cfm.

Johnson, D. W. & Johnson, R. T. (1994). *Learning Together and Alone: Cooperative, Competitive, and Individualistic Learning.* Needham Heights, MA: Allyn & Bacon.

Johnson-Laird, P. & Byrne, R. (2000). Mental Models Website: A Gentle Introduction. Retrieved May 6, 2005, from http://www.tcd.ie/Psychology/Ruth_Byrne/mental_models/index.html.

Kruse, S. D., Louis, K. S., & Bryk, A. (1995). An emerging framework for analyzing school-based professional community. In K. S. Louis and S. D. Kruse (Eds.), *Professionalism and Community: Perspectives on Reforming Urban Schools, (pp. 23–42).* Thousand Oaks, CA: Corwin.

LaPlant, L. & Zane, N. (2005). Partner learning systems. In J. S. Thousand, R. A. Villa, & A. I. Nevin. (Eds.), *Creativity and Collaborative Learning: The Practical Guide to Empowering Students, Teachers, and Families,* (pp. 271–282). Baltimore: Brookes.

Leask, M. & Younie, S. (2001). The European Schoolnet. An online European community for teachers? A valuable professional resource? *Teacher Development, 5*(2), 157–175.

Mills, G. E. (2000). *Action Research: A Guide for the Teacher Researcher.* Upper Saddle River, NJ: Merrill.

Mouza , C. (2002). Learning to teach with new technology: Implications for professional development. *Journal of Research on Technology in Education, 35*(2), 272–289.

Ohio Department of Education. (2002). Transforming learning communities: A research project on school change. Retrieved April 28, 2005, from http://www.ode.state.oh.us/tlc/.

O'Neil, J. (1995). On schools as learning organizations: A conversation with Peter Senge. *Educational Leadership, 52*(7), 20–23.

Patton, M. Q. (2002). *Qualitative research and evaluation methods.* Thousand Oaks, CA: Sage.

Reynolds, E., Treahy, D., Chao, C. C., & Barab, S. (2001). The Internet Learning Forum: Developing a community prototype for teachers of the 21st century. *Computers in the Schools, 17*(3–4), 107–125.

Roberts, S. M. & Pruitt, E. Z. (2003). *Schools as Professional Learning Communities: Collaborative Activities and Strategies for Professional Development.* Thousand Oaks, CA: Corwin.

School Change Collaborative. (2005). Development of materials to support the formation of learning communities. Retrieved April 15, 2005, from http://www.nwrel.org/scpd/scc/natspec/formlc.shtml.

Senge, P. M. (1990). *The Fifth Discipline: The Art and Practice of the Learning Organization.* New York: Doubleday.

Senge, P., Cambron-McCabe, N., Lucas, T., Smith, B., Dutton, J., & Kleiner, A. (2000). *Schools that learn: A Fifth Discipline Fieldbook for Educators, Parents, and Everyone Who Cares About Education.* New York: Doubleday.

Smith, M. K. (2001). Peter Senge and the learning organization. *The Encyclopedia of Informal Education.* Retrieved April 15, 2005, from http://www.infed.org/thinkers/senge.htm.

Stinnette, L. J., Peterson, K., & Hallinger P. (2005). Becoming a community of learners: Emerging leadership practices. Retrieved April 30, 2005, from http://www.ncrel.org/cscd/pubs/lead21/2-11.htm.

Thousand, J. S., Villa, R. A., & Nevin, A. I. (2005). *Creativity and Collaborative Learning: The Practical Guide to Empowering Students, Teachers, and Families.* Baltimore: Brookes.

Topper, A. G., Gillingham, M. G., Ellefson, N. C., & Worthington, V. L. (1997). Teacher professional development on the World Wide Web: The LETSNet web site and teacher learning. *Journal of Computing in Teacher Education, 13*(4), 25–33.

Villalobos, P. J., Eshilian, L., & Moyer, J. (2005). Empowering secondary students to take the lead: Training activities to promote advocacy, inclusion, and social justice. In J. S. Thousand, R. A. Villa, & A. I. Nevin. (Eds.), *Creativity and Collaborative Learning: The Practical Guide to Empowering Students, Teachers, and Families,* (pp. 431–464). Baltimore: Brookes.

Zmuda, A., Kuklis, R., & Kline, E. (2004). *Transforming Schools: Creating a Culture of Continuous Improvement.* Alexandria, VA: Association for Supervision and Curriculum Development.

Professional Development of Teacher-Leader/Designers

National Board for Professional Teaching Standards

This chapter will discuss the National Board for Professional Teaching Standards (NBPTS) and the professional development opportunities that NBPTS provide for the Teacher-Leader/Designer. In addition, the history of NBPTS, the necessary requirements, and the assessment process used by NBPTS, will be described, as well as what it means within the teaching profession to be a National Board certified teacher.

After reading this chapter, you will be able to:

1. Define National Board for Professional Teaching Standards (NBPTS).
2. Explain how Teacher-Leader/Designers aligns with NBPTS.
3. Provide the history and purpose of NBPTS.
4. Identify the five core propositions of NBPTS.
5. Describe the requirements and process of NBPTS.
6. Describe the incentives for achieving NBPTS.
7. Describe the impact of NBPTS on teachers' behaviors.
8. Describe the impact of NBPTS on students' behaviors.

WHAT IS THE RELATIONSHIP BETWEEN THE TEACHER-LEADER/DESIGNER AND NATIONAL BOARDS?

Many teachers who are Teacher-Leader/Designers seek opportunities for professional growth and development. After a period of successful teaching, teachers often seek opportunities that will help to rejuvenate and continue to motivate them in the classroom (Huberman, 1989). According to behavioral theorist Fredrick Herzberg (1966), motivating issues include recognition, achievement, advancement, growth, responsibility, and job challenge. The need for personal achievement and public recognition is especially true for teachers (Sergiovanni & Carver, 1973). Teachers need professional development opportunities to talk publicly about their learning, work, and classroom practices (Lieberman, 1995). For many years, obtaining a graduate degree in education was the only formal avenue teachers had for professional development, personal achievement, and public recognition and reward for advancing their teaching credentials while remaining active in the classroom.

Today, along with obtaining a graduate degree in teaching, teachers can now pursue National Board Certification for professional development (Guskey, 1997). The process for obtaining National Board Certification includes growth, responsibility, and job challenge. Nationally Board Certified teachers receive recognition. For many Teacher-Leader/Designers, seeking and achieving National Board Certification is a logical step for them to take because they are implementing the practices that the National Board recognizes as important for teachers. The majority of National Board Certified teachers view "serving in leadership roles" as an important professional activity for implementation (Dagenhart, 2002). But what exactly is the National Board, how did it develop, how can one earn certification, and what does it mean to be a National Board Certified teacher?

WHAT ARE NATIONAL BOARD FOR PROFESSIONAL TEACHING STANDARDS?

National Board for Professional Teaching Standards (NBPTS) are a National Board Certification that is a mark of professionalism, validates good teaching, impacts student learning in a positive way, provides a measure for teacher quality, and creates mentor and other professional opportunities (Castor, 2002). The underlying philosophy of NBPTS is the strong belief that quality teachers are essential for student achievement. The National Board was developed by teachers, with teachers, and for teachers. In short, NBPTS is a symbol of teaching excellence.

NBPTS is an independent, nonprofit, nonpartisan organization governed by a board of directors, the majority of whom are classroom teachers (NBPTS, 2001a). Other members include school administrators, school board members, governors and state legislators, higher education officials, teacher union leaders, and business and community leaders. With the belief that improving teaching is the key to improving our national level of student achievement, NBPTS is dedicated to establishing and upholding high standards for professional performance.

The NBPTS mission is to advance the quality of teaching and learning (NBPTS, 2001b). It is believed this mission can be accomplished in the following ways. First, the NBPTS believes it is critical within the teaching profession for teachers to maintain high and rigorous standards for themselves. Second, it is necessary for a national voluntary system to be in place to certify teachers who meet such standards. Third, the NBPTS advocates that related education reforms in America should consult, integrate, and tap into the expertise of National Board Certification.

THE HISTORY AND PURPOSE OF NBPTS

The federal report, *A Nation at Risk*, published in 1983 caused quite a stir in this country and resulted in many educational reforms. In 1986, the Carnegie Task Force on Teaching produced a report entitled, *A Nation Prepared: Teachers for the 21st Century*, which stated that teachers need to have a set of rigorous standards similar to those of other professional fields. Based on the strong recommendations from this report, the NBPTS was established in 1987.

The purpose of NBPTS is to exemplify the best in teaching by defining high standards and to encourage all teachers to meet these clearly defined standards. Because the NBPTS is so widely recognized and held in such high esteem, many accomplished teachers seek to achieve this distinction. National Boards is offered to individuals on a voluntary basis and is designed to complement, not replace, state licensing (NBPTS, 2001a). The NBPTS targets experienced teachers meeting entry-level standards set by each state. In 1989, the NBPTS published its policy statement, *What Teachers Should Know and Be Able to Do*, which has been the primary guide for teachers and institutions with the objective of improving the teaching profession.

FIVE CORE PROPOSITIONS OF THE NBPTS

The NBPTS seeks to identify and recognize teachers who are effective Leaders and Designers in their classrooms. When teachers emerge as Teacher-Leader/Designers in the classroom, their behavior and the choices they make in the classroom are often aligned with the NBPTS' five core propositions. These core propositions are published in the monograph, *What Teachers Should Know and Be Able to Do* (NBPTS, 1989). Each of the propositions are stated and described in the following paragraphs.

The first proposition is *Teachers are committed to students and their learning.* First and foremost, teachers must believe that students can learn and must understand how students develop and learn. Accomplished teachers treat all students equitably, recognize their differences, and are able to differentiate instructional practices when necessary. The culture and heritage of all students are respected, and teachers foster students' self-esteem and motivation for learning.

The second proposition is *Teachers know the subjects they teach and how to teach those subjects.* It is important that board-certified teachers are knowledgeable of the content they teach, how the content is organized, how the content is connected to other content, and how to effectively integrate content and connect it to the real world. In addition to having a wide range of instructional strategies, board-certified teachers help students become problem solvers and develop higher thinking skills.

The third proposition is *Teachers are responsible for managing and monitoring student learning.* Time management is an important tool for board-certified teachers. They are always cognizant of the importance of effective use of instructional time and are able to maintain high levels of student time-on-task during the instructional time. Teachers create a nurturing classroom environment by providing an inviting atmosphere for learning with the expectation that all students will demonstrate appropriate behavior for the classroom. The board-certified teacher is able to successfully assess the progress of the class as well as the progress of individual students through a variety of assessment tools. Frequent communication with parents regarding the progress of their child is conducted by the teacher.

The fourth proposition is *Teachers think systematically about their practice and learn from experience.* Board-certified teachers incorporate reflection into their practice and are able to make sound judgments based on reasoning. These teachers are skilled at taking multiple perspectives of situations and circumstances and, based on these multiple perspectives, make professional judgements. Board-certified teachers possess the confidence to take risks and to take creative approaches in implementing the curriculum for their students. In addition, these teachers are highly effective problem solvers. Regardless of the outcomes of their decisions, teachers realize that they will learn something valuable from their experiences. These teachers believe in the concept of lifelong learning and are always eager to learn something new and interesting. This eagerness to learn is an important trait to model for their students. Board-certified teachers continuously strive to improve their teaching through systematic and disciplined behavior.

The fifth and final proposition is *Teachers are members of learning communities.* Board-certified teachers contribute to the overall effectiveness of their school through leadership and design by working collaboratively with other professionals on instructional policy, curriculum development, and staff development. They are able to evaluate school progress and the allocation of school resources using their working knowledge and understanding of state educational objectives. Board-certified teachers are knowledgeable about resource availability from the local, state, national, and international levels and about how to acquire and utilize these resources for the benefit of their students. These accomplished teachers are able to work collaboratively and constructively with parents and others outside of the school who have a stake in the education of the children.

WHAT ARE THE REQUIREMENTS AND PROCESS FOR BECOMING AN NBPTS TEACHER?

There are some basic requirements to becoming an NBPTS teacher. First, candidates must hold a baccalaureate degree with a minimum of three years of teaching experience while holding a valid state teaching license. This teaching experience can be either in a public or private school. Once these basic requirements are met, the teacher is able to formally apply to receive National Board Certification status and become Nationally Board Certified.

The National Board Certification test application consists of a demonstration of the candidate's knowledge and skills through a series of performance-based assessments. This performance-based assessment is a two-step process and takes approximately 200 to 400 hours (NBPTS, 2001a). This performance-based assessment includes a professional portfolio, which consists of four entries that are based on a candidate's classroom practice. The portfolio contains various products, including examples of student work, videotapes of the candidate teaching, and other instructional artifacts. The videos and student work are supported by narratives and commentaries from the candidates on the goals and purposes of instruction, reflections on what occurred and the effectiveness of the practice, and the rationale for the candidate's professional judgment.

The portfolio is submitted to the NBPTS and is scored by highly qualified teachers who have been specifically trained in scoring the portfolio based on the National Board Standards. In addition to the portfolio, candidates are required to take and pass one-day exercises. These exercises are to be taken at a designated NBPTS assessment center located throughout the United States. These exercises allow the candidates the opportunity to demonstrate their professional knowledge and content knowledge within a selected content area.

WHAT ARE THE INCENTIVES TO BECOMING AN NBPTS TEACHER?

A Nationally Board Certified teacher is held in high regard across the nation, and there are incentives for certification in at least forty-four states (Vandevoort, Amrein-Beardsley, & Berliner, 2004). Many of these incentives include financial rewards, whereas other incentives include the intrinsic reward of knowing that highly qualified peers identify you as a master teacher (Bond, et al., 2000). This recognition of this certification is held in high esteem by colleagues, administrators, parents, community members, and legislators. Teachers who have participated in National Board Certification have overwhelmingly acknowledged that it is the most powerful professional development experience of their career (O'Connor, 2003). Teachers have stated that during the certification process, "they deepen their content knowledge and develop, master, and reflect on new approaches to working with their students" (North Carolina Department of Public Instruction, 2002).

A research study was commissioned by NBPTS in 2001 to examine the effects of preparation and obtaining National Board Certification status for teachers. The majority of teachers stated that participation in the process has had a greater impact on them than actually achieving the certificate. The study also found that board-certified teachers brought new instructional techniques and activities into their classrooms, resulting in increased effectiveness in the classroom. A board-certified teacher tends to achieve other leadership opportunities at the school, community, and state level. Betty Castor, former NBPTS president, comments that National Board Certified Teachers (NBCTs) are taking on leadership roles from within the classroom. Castor states, "The Challenge now is to further integrate them (sic) (NBCTs) into the decision-making process, ensuring that their growing leadership capabilities do not go untapped" (NBPTS, 2001a, p. 1). Whether it is mentoring new teachers, serving as a student teacher supervisor, or developing instructional materials, NBCTs, in the capacity of leadership roles, are strengthening the overall teaching profession (O'Connor, 2003).

SUMMARY

There is a natural relationship between Teacher-Leader/Designers and teachers who achieve National Board Certification. Teacher-Leader/Designers and board-certified teachers are the teachers who believe in the teaching profession and recognize the key for improving and transforming schools is to implement ongoing professional development programs for teachers. Linda Darling-Hammond (1996) stated, "Studies show that teachers' ability, experience, and education are clearly associated with increases in student achievement. Spending additional resources on teacher professional development is the most productive investment schools can make to raise student achievement" (p. 5–6).

The NBPTS uses standards for accomplished teaching as the impetus for changing teachers and their behaviors in the classroom. The NBPTS is achieving its goal of creating standards to guide the teaching profession and assess teachers who utilize such standards. Equally important, Teacher-Leader/Designers seek National Board Certification as a means to professional growth and development. Teachers who go through the NBPTS process and achieve the distinction of becoming Nationally Board Certified state that they are more skillful in the classroom because they possess a deeper knowledge of content, are better assessors of students growth, develop better leadership skills, and believe in themselves more as professionals. Thus, it is highly appropriate to label teachers who elect to achieve NBPTS recognition, as well as teachers who elect to earn a graduate degree in education, as exemplary examples of Teacher-Leader/Designers.

CASE STUDY

Ms. Butler is an elementary teacher of students with moderate mental retardation. She has been teaching for over seven years and has already earned her master's degree in special education. She is a hard working and conscientious teacher who truly believes in her students and the difference that she makes in their lives. Ms. Butler decides to seek her National Board Certification. She was not discouraged by the negative comments she received from her colleagues who described the National Board certification process as too difficult, with most people failing to pass. She believes that regardless of the pass/fail outcome, she will benefit personally and professionally in her pursuit of National Board Certification.

Ms. Butler just received notification today that she did indeed pass the requirements of National Board Certification. Needless to say, she is elated! When asked to reflect upon this experience, she said,

> "Well, first of all, this experience not only changed my teaching and my views of education, it changed my life! I feel more confident in my ability as a teacher. I now see the education system in a global sense. Because of the requirements for National Boards, I was forced to really think about and analyze my actions that I took in the classroom. I realized for the first time, even though they have always been available, the value of using surveys to collect data, employing different assessment tools on my students, how to use technology more effectively, and the other people in my school as resources. It helped me see the importance of reaching all of my parents and forming close relationships with them and my students. In fact, this experience has exceeded all expectations! I know that I am a better teacher and person because of the National Board Certification process. I will help others by sharing my experience and encouraging others to go for it!"

ACTIVITIES

1. Visit the NBPTS website and find the research and information link. Locate two research studies and critique the research. What research study would you like to see conducted in relation to NBPTS?

2. Design and implement an informal survey with people from a varied population (colleagues, community members, students, etc.) to learn what they know about NBPTS. If they are aware of NBPTS, what are their opinions about NBPTS and the certification process?

DISCUSSION QUESTIONS

1. How do you think the National Board Certification process would affect an individual's teaching ability?

2. Do you think that having National Board Certification will affect teachers' professional life outside the classroom? If so, how?

3. Do you think members of your school community (colleagues, administrators, parents, etc.) recognize the value of National Board Certification? Why or why not?

REFERENCES

Bond, L., Smith, T. W., Baker, W. K., & Hattie, J. A. (2000, Sept). *The certification system of the National Board for Professional Teaching Standards: A construct and consequential validity study.* Study conducted by the Center for Educational Research and Evaluation, University of North Carolina, Greensboro.

Carnegie Forum on Education and Economy (1986, May). *A nation prepared: Teachers for the 21st Century, the report of the Task Force on Teaching as a Profession.* Washington, DC: Author.

Castor, B. (2002, Spring). National board certification: A measure of quality. *The Professional Standard, 2*(2), 39–46.

Dagenhart, D. B. (2002). *Comparing the wants and needs of National Board Certified with non–National Board Certified middle school teachers for personal job success and satisfaction.* Dissertation submitted to the faculty of the University of North Carolina, Chapel Hill.

Darling-Hammond, L. (1996). *What matters most: Teaching for America's future.* Woodbridge, VA: National Commission on Teaching and America's Future.

Guskey, T. R. (1997). Research needs link professional development and student learning. *Journal of Staff Development, 18*(2), 36–40.

Herzberg, F. (1966). *Work and the Nature of Man.* New York: World.

Huberman, M. (1989). The professional life cycle of teachers. *Teachers College Record, 91*(1), 31–57.

Liebermann, A. (Ed.). (1995). *The Work of Restructuring Schools: Building from the Ground Up.* New York: Teachers College Press.

National Board for Professional Teaching Standards. (1989). *What Teachers Should Know and Be Able to Do.* Arlington, VA: Author.

National Board for Professional Teaching Standards. (2001a). *Guide to National Board Certification.* Oxford, UK: Harcourt Educational Management.

National Board for Professional Teaching Standards. (2001b). *I am a better teacher: What candidates for National Board Certification say about the assessment process.* An NBPTS research report. Available online at http://www.nbpts.org/pdf/better_teacher.pdf.

North Carolina Department of Public Instruction. (2002). *North Carolina: Home to 5,137 National Board Teachers.* Available online at http://www.ncpublicschools.org/nbpts/.

O'Connor, K. A. (2003). *Identifying the wants and needs of North Carolina upper elementary (grades 3–5) National Board and non-National Board certified teachers for job success and satisfaction.* Dissertation submitted to the faculty of the University of North Carolina, Chapel Hill.

Sergiovanni, T. & Carver, F. (1973). *The New School Executive: A Theory of Administration.* New York: Harper and Row.

Vandevoort, L. G., Amrein-Beardsley, A., & Berliner, D. C. (2004). National board certified teachers and their students' achievement. *Education Policy Analysis Archives, 12,* (46), 1–45.

Chapter 12

Teacher-Leader/ Designers Are Reflective Practitioners

This chapter will define reflection and reflective practitioner, as well as the role and importance of reflection for a Teacher-Leader/Designer, and how to reflect appropriately as a Teacher-Leader/Designer. This chapter will also describe why reflection is important and how it benefits the reflector. How reflection is an essential component of several professional organizations will be explored and discussed.

After reading this chapter, you will be able to:

1. Define teacher reflection.
2. Describe the reflective process.
3. Express the importance of teacher reflection.
4. Reflect in an appropriate manner.
5. Describe how reflection impacts teaching.
6. Know when to reflect.
7. Know where to reflect.
8. Provide an example of reflection.
9. Discuss the role of reflection in professional development.

WHAT IS REFLECTION?

Teachers are required to make diagnoses; develop and revise plans; implement lessons; provide meaningful experiences; nurture; communicate with learners, parents, and other teachers; involve all learners; and more (Manning & Payne, 1996). On average, teachers have 1000 face-to-face interactions per day (Jackson, 1968), make critical decisions approximately every two minutes (Clark & Peterson, 1986), and lose 55 percent of their instructional time to disruption (Gottfredson, 1990). Such statistics illustrate the complexity inherent in teaching. They also emphasize the mental alertness, awareness, monitoring, and evaluation necessary to effective teaching and learning in the classroom. Such mental processes, especially the evaluation aspect, are what we mean by reflection.

It is challenging to describe the reflection process of Teacher-Leader/Designers because much of it is contained in their thought processes and cannot be observed directly. Reflection is the cyclical process of assessing information, thinking about and analyzing data, and using the conclusions to modify or change future actions. Dewey (1910) described reflective thinking as a state of hesitation that includes "the act of searching, hunting, inquiring to find material that will resolve the doubt, settle and dispose of the perplexity" (p. 12). Learning to reflect more effectively is a process that continues well after the first year of teaching. As a matter of fact, it continues throughout one's career. Active reflection is what keeps teaching interesting!

What is critical reflection? Scholars have written volumes about critical reflection and each scholar appears to have a unique definition or interpretation for reflection, critical reflection, self-reflection, reflection-on-action, and reflection-in-action depending on their school of learning. Mezirow (1995) provides the following definition for reflection and critical reflection.

> Intentional construal is required to transform our meaning schemes and perspectives. We do this through *reflection* [emphasis in original], understood here as an apperceptive assessment of the justification for our beliefs, ideas, or feelings. Ordinary reflection involves intentional assessment of the nature and consequences of these learnings. The kind of reflection [sic] which includes and relates the circumstances of their origin with their nature and consequences can be understood as *critical reflection* [emphasis in original] (pp. 44–45).

A thirty-five year veteran teacher shared with her mentee, a first-year teacher, that what kept her excited about teaching after so many years of being in the classroom was that there was still so much to learn and think about regarding teaching. It is astounding, even after thirty-five years in the classroom, that a veteran realized that she still had much to learn about teaching and was constantly thinking of ways to be more effective with her students. In teaching, there is always so much to learn, so much to explore, so many exciting challenges, and so many opportunities regardless of your teaching experience. True Teacher-Leader/Designers are constantly striving to refine and improve their practice of teaching, and much of that is done through their reflection.

THE IMPORTANCE OF REFLECTION

Reflection is considered an essential aspect of being an effective teacher (Bullock & Hawk, 2003). In teaching, it is the thought that counts! This statement does not mean that thinking is more important than actions. Rather, it means that teachers must be thinkers and decision makers who take full responsibility for their classrooms and students, and this process occurs through reflection (Shalaway, 1989). The best way for teachers to grow professionally is to assume more responsibility for their own learning and teaching (Payne & Manning, 1995). A key to teachers taking charge of their own thinking is to become more reflective. When teachers become "thinking individuals" about their profession, they are empowered in the classroom and beyond. Teachers should construct meaning about themselves through reflection (O'Connor, 2003).

Don Schon (1983) helped pioneer the concept of "reflective practitioner." He stated that when a situation is examined, individuals tend to be influenced by what has happened earlier or what may happen next. Changing over time involves thinking about one's personal and professional frameworks (O'Connor, 2003). Mezirow (1978) refers to this change in values and beliefs as the transformation process which he developed into his transformational theory. According to Mezirow (1996), "Transformation Theory is an evolving theory of adult learning . . . grounded in the nature of human communication . . . [in which] learning is understood as the process of using a prior interpretation to construe a new or revised interpretation of the meaning of one's experiences in order to guide future action" (p. 162).

An example of the reflective process is that a teacher may think (reflect) about a certain situation, develop strategies to conquer the situation (renewal), and then take action on the situation (growth) (Steffy, et al., 2000). As a Chinese proverb states, "The definition of insanity is doing the same action over and over and expecting different results."

As stated earlier, reflecting on what occurs in the classroom is key to professional growth for teachers. An increased awareness of one's actions and the consequences of those actions often are not realized and understood until the individual takes time to pause and think about it (Lichtenstein, 2000). When to reflect will be discussed later in this chapter. Reflection is what allows us to learn from our experiences and grow. The reflective process is an assessment of where we have been and where we want to go next in our professional journey of teaching.

HOW TO REFLECT

There is no one correct and official reflection process; the process varies according to individual needs and style. What is important with reflecting is that it is conducted in a systematic fashion. However, for this chapter,

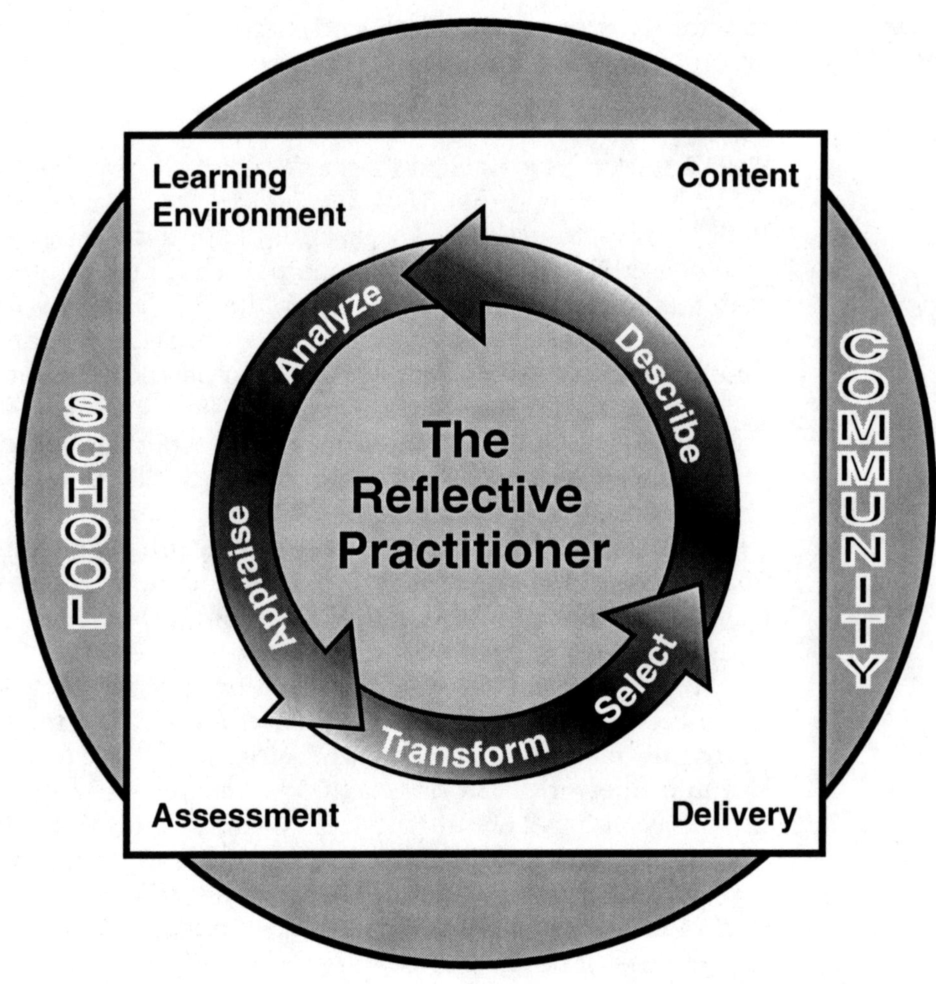

Figure 12-1

one example of the reflection process will be provided (see Figure 12.1). Each of the five steps will be discussed in proper sequence.

The first step is to select a piece of evidence or experience to reflect upon; for example, student work, a student test, or a parent-teacher conference. When you select a piece of evidence or experience, you then need to determine if there are any additional artifacts or evidence that support your selection. If there are, they need to be included as well. Next, you will need to discuss why you selected the particular evidence or experience you selected.

The second step is to describe the piece of evidence or experience. This description involves the *Who, What, When,* and *Where* questions. To answer *Who,* one needs to include the individuals involved and clearly identify their roles. *What* explains what is being examined. Of course, *When* provides the time frame, and *Where* provides the location and setting. Each of these descriptors is important in providing the details, circumstance, and parameters of what is being examined, evaluated, and reflected upon.

The third step is the analysis of the piece of evidence or experience. This step of analysis is where one provides answers to *Why* and *How.* Responding to *How* allows the reader to understand how this particular piece of evidence or experience was selected and *Why* provides the reader with insights on what prompted the individual to select the particular piece of evidence or experience.

The fourth step is where the teacher appraises the piece of evidence or experience. This step of appraising includes interpreting an event, determining its impact, determining its effectiveness, and determining its relationship to goals, values, and philosophy. It is evident that the fourth step involves a great deal of the thought process and thus is a critical component of reflection.

The fifth step, known as the transform step, is where the reflection process impacts future behavior in the classroom. In this step, one utilizes the information and data collected, applies them to the teaching practice, and develops new goals and strategies based on that data.

HOW REFLECTIVE PRACTICES IMPACT TEACHERS

The reflection process is critical to the development of Teacher-Leader/Designers. Through reflection, teachers are able to better integrate the art and science of teaching with the aspects of leadership and designing. The integration of those four components occurs because reflection is an ongoing, cyclical process. Reflection requires careful and thoughtful reporting and analysis of one's teaching practice, philosophy, and experience (Lashley, 1992). The ability to examine, evaluate, and understand whether a teaching strategy or action taken in the classroom was effective is important for professional growth to occur.

Brookfield (1995) carries the reflection process a step further by requiring the practitioner to engage in critical reflection. He provides six reasons for the importance for teachers to engage in critical reflection and to develop a critical rationale for the professional practice. Critical reflection allows the practitioner to take informed actions, to develop a rationale for practice, to avoid self-laceration, to ground the teacher emotionally, to enliven the classroom, and to increase democratic trust. Critical reflection leads to justice, fairness, and compassion in the democratic and learner-centered classroom in which each student is respected, valued for contributions and heard by the teacher.

Personal emotions are an important variable in the thought process and therefore in the learning process. Jennifer Moon, in *Reflection in Learning and Professional Development* (1999), discusses Mezirow as an exception to the norm while exploring the role of emotion, an affective function, in the reflective process (p. 94). She continues, "the nature of the role of emotion is rarely addressed directly" (p. 95). Patton (2004) builds a case for interpreting Mezirow's transformation theory as a holistic theory through Mezirow's acknowledgement of the role of emotion in personal development, growth, and learning. Mezirow's (1994) transformation theory includes the following 11 phases:

> (1) a disorienting dilemma, (2) self-examination with feelings of guilt or shame, *sometimes turning to religion for support* [italics added], (3) a criti-

> cal assessment of assumptions, (4) recognition that one's discontent and the process of transformation are shared and that others have negotiated a similar change, (5) exploration of options for new roles, relationships, and actions, (6) planning of a course of action, (7) acquiring knowledge and skills for implementing one's plans, (8) provisionally trying out new roles, (9) *renegotiating relationships and negotiating new relationships* [italics added], (10) building competence and self-confidence in new roles and relationships, and (11) a reintegration into one's life on the basis of conditions dictated by one's new perspective (p. 224).

Critical reflection and critical assessment of assumptions, beliefs and values lead to growth in personal development for both teachers and learners of all ages.

The reflection process provides a focus for teachers. When teachers ask themselves consistently and systematically why they do what they do with their students, and their rationale for doing it, it allows teachers to always be assessing their thoughts, actions, and deeds, and consequently will impact future behavior. In the reflection process, it is often helpful for teachers to have some guiding questions that they address as they reflect on a piece of evidence or experience. Examples of some guiding questions might be the following: Based on this experience, what have I learned about my teaching? What have I leaned about my students? What changes will I make as a result? How is student learning impacted? Of course, there are a multitude of questions that can be used to guide the reflection process.

AN EXAMPLE OF TEACHER REFLECTION

The following example describes a teacher reflecting about differentiating instruction and student development within her third-grade classroom. This example provides only a section of her reflection process, but it captures the flavor of her thinking through and reflecting about what works best for her students. As this third-grade teacher reflects about her spelling lessons, it will impact her future actions in the classroom.

> *In addition to the third-grade spelling list, I have implemented an additional spelling program which causes the students to assume more responsibility for identifying and using learning resources. Students gather words from various places, such as misspelled words from their writing, words around the room, and vocabulary words. Students are responsible for accumulating words to form their list, and they use dictionaries, computers, and encyclopedias to find the correct spellings and meanings of their words.*
>
> *I learned that having students be more responsible for their learning and choosing their own spelling words allows those who are strong spellers to continue to improve, while those who are weak spellers can get the practice on the words they commonly use and misspell in their writing. I learned that I can count on most of the students to challenge themselves without my having to constantly be teaching them and guiding their activities. There are*

some students who try to take advantage of a system like this, and I can not always trust them to do as they are told.

This third-grade teacher is changing her behavior in the classroom based on the reflection process she underwent concerning a spelling for her students. Through careful and thoughtful analysis of her teaching, this third-grade teacher was able to reflect on her students' development and how to use multiple instructional strategies more effectively in the classroom. This, in turn, will allow her to try a different approach, which she hopes will be more effective.

WHERE, WHEN, AND HOW TO REFLECT

Being a reflective practitioner requires time, practice, and environmental support (O'Connor, 2003). This is a highly individualized process and teachers have to discover for themselves what works best for them. Once a pattern of *Where, When* and *How* is established, reflecting often becomes an indispensable and routine habit for teachers.

For many teachers, *When* to reflect is often connected to the experience and the opportunity. The ideal time to reflect is immediately after the lesson or experience. This is a time when the events are fresh in one's mind and one is able to remember the lesson or experience in greater detail. However, in most cases, teachers have to move on to the next lesson or event planned for the day, which often forces them to find some other uninterrupted time to reflect.

Some teachers prefer to reflect in the setting in which they teach. For some teachers, finding a time to reflect in their classroom could mean arriving at school a little earlier in the morning before the students arrive. The morning is generally a time when one is fresh and is able to think clearly. Other teachers find time to reflect during their planning period. However, the planning period is often committed to miscellaneous items that need to be taken care of.

The only other time for teachers to reflect at school occurs at the end of the school day. That time, like the planning period, is often used for various meetings and other related school activities. However, some teachers choose to wait until after those school obligations are met before they begin to reflect. When teachers wait for this time of the school day to reflect, they often have the luxury of not being rushed because of time constraints.

The reflection process is not restricted to the classroom. Some teachers find other places within the school in which to reflect; for example, the library, a conference room, or even the lounge.

Reflecting certainly does not have to occur only on the school grounds. Teachers can engage in the reflective process in many different places, in numerous ways, and at various times. Because much of the reflecting process is a basic cognitive activity (Muth & Alvermann, 2000), reflecting can occur in the car while commuting to work or doing errands. Also, some teachers find that they are able to reflect while doing household chores. For example, while washing dishes, a teacher may think about the science experiment that had occurred earlier that day in her classroom and reflect upon what went well and what did not go as well as expected. When the teacher formally writes her reflection on the science experiment, she has had the opportunity to think and ponder over the experience and the possible meanings of the events.

The *Where* (place and time) can vary and so can the *How*. Because much of the reflection process is a mental activity, teachers often need methods that help them to express in words, to remember, and to organize their thoughts. For most teachers, the computer is the most popular way to write a formal reflection process cycle, whereas others use sticky notes, video or audio tapes, or even a recording device.

As one can see, the reflective process can occur in many settings and at many times. The key is for teachers to experiment and find what combination of place and time that works best for them. Everyone is different, so each individual's reflecting process will be somewhat idiosyncratic.

SUMMARY

Reflection is a critical component of what Teacher-Leader/Designers do for their professional growth. Reflection is a systematic, cognitive, and cyclical process that allows teachers to grow professionally through their assessments of what has occurred in their classroom and beyond. The reflective process provides a mechanism for teachers to learn from their professional events and experiences and will impact their future thoughts, actions, and deeds in the teaching profession.

CASE STUDY

Mr. Nyuag is teaching a tenth-grade biology class as a first-year teacher. He soon realized that he was not prepared for the diverse needs of his multicultural class. At the end of each school day, Mr. Nyuag felt frustrated because he believed that he was not "reaching" his students. In other words, he sensed that there was a communication barrier. He went to his mentor, Ms. Wright and asked for help in this matter. Ms. Wright recommended that he use the reflection cycle to help him identify specific areas that could be addressed. He followed Ms. Wright's advice and found through reflecting that he was not as sensitive to the beliefs and customs of his students as perhaps he could be. For example, he noted that one of his students was from Sri Lanka who had been taught not to make direct eye contact because it is disrespectful. In addition, this student had many religious dietary restrictions. He had incorrectly interpreted that this student was being disrespectful and difficult. Through the reflective process, Mr. Nyuag felt that he was able to be proactive in improving his teaching performance and not reactive.

ACTIVITIES

1. Select a lesson that you have taught and reflect with the following guiding questions. What went well with the lesson? Why did you use the teaching strategies you selected for this lesson? Was the lesson's objective(s) achieved by the students? How do you know the objective(s) were achieved? If you had to reteach this lesson, what would you do differently?

2. After attending a workshop or an inservice meeting, respond to the following questions. What were the best materials of the workshop? What things did you learn? What did you agree and disagree with?

DISCUSSION QUESTIONS

1. Is it possible for a teacher not to engage in the reflective process and still be effective in the classroom? Why or why not?

2. Should the reflective process be taught to preservice and beginning teachers, or should they learn it on their own? Why or why not?

REFERENCES

Brookfield, S. (1995). *Becoming a critically reflective teacher.* San Francisco: Jossey Bass.

Bullock, A. A. & Hawk, P. P. (2003). *Developing a Teaching Portfolio.* (2nd ed.). Upper Saddle River, NJ: Merrill Prentice-Hall.

Clark, C. M. & Peterson, P. L. (1986). Teacher's thought process. In M. Wittrock (Ed.), *Handbook of Research on Teaching* (3rd ed.). New York: Macmillan.

Dewey, J. (1910). *How We Think.* New York: Heath.

Gottfredson, D. C. (1990). Developing effective organizations to reduce school disorder. In O. C. Moles (Ed.), *Student Discipline Strategies: Research and Practice,* (pp. 47–62). Albany: State University of New York Press.

Jackson, P. W. (1968). *Life in Classrooms.* New York: Holt, Rinehart, and Winston.

Lashley, T. (1992). Promoting teacher reflection. *Journal of Staff Development, 13*(1), 24–29.

Lichtenstein, B. B. (2000). Generating knowledge and self-organized learning: Reflecting on Don Schon's research. *Journal of Management Inquiry, 9,* 47–54.

Manning, B. H. & Payne, B. D. (1996). *Self-Talk for Teachers and Students.* Needham Heights, MA: Allyn & Bacon.

Mezirow, J. (1978). Perspective transformation. *Adult Education, 28* (2), 100–110.

Mezirow, J. (1995). Transformation theory of adult learning. In M. R. Welton (ed.), *In defense of the lifeworld: Critical perspectives on adult learning.* New York: State University of New York Press.

Mezirow, J. (1996). Contemporary paradigms of learning. *Adult Education Quarterly, 46* (3), 158–172.

Moon, J. A. (1999). *Reflection in learning & professional development: Theory & practice.* Sterling, VA: Stylus Publishing, Inc.

Muth, K. D. & Alvermann, D. E. (2000). *Teaching and Learning in the Middle Grades* (2nd ed.). Boston: Allyn & Bacon.

North Carolina Department of Public Instruction. (1996). *The Reflection Cycle.* Raleigh, NC: Performance-Based Licensure Project.

Patton, B. L. (2004). Unpublished manuscript. *Cocaine is to mistress as adultery is to divorce: An analogy for perspective tranformation.* East Carolina University, Greenville, NC.

Payne, B. D. & Manning, B. H. (1991). Cognitive self-direction methodological model. *Teacher Education Quarterly, 18*(1), 49–54.

O'Connor, K. A. (2003). Identifying the wants and needs of North Carolina upper elementary (grades 3–5) national board and non–national board teachers for job success and satisfaction. Dissertation submitted to the faculty of the University of North Carolina, Chapel Hill.

Schon, D. A. (1983). *The Reflective Practitioner: How Professionals Think in Action.* New York: Basic.

Shalaway, L. (1989). *Learning to Teach.* New York: Scholastic.

Steffy, B. E., Wolfe, M. P., Pasch, S. H., & Enz, B. J. (2000). *Life Cycle of the Career Teacher.* Thousand Oaks, CA: Corwin.